W9-BAS-819

OCT 3 0 2003

8-1-10(12)
12-19-11(14)
2.22.12(16)
12-6-17(25)

Fostoria

Fine Crystal and Colored Glassware
Cut, Etched and Plain

**REPRINT OF A
SUPPLEMENTARY CATALOG
1925-1930**

© 2000

L-W BOOK SALES
PO Box 69
Gas City, IN 46933

ISBN# 0-89538-113-3

Published by: L-W Book Sales
                  PO Box 69
                  Gas City, IN 46933

Please write L-W BOOKS for our free catalog
of books on antiques and collectibles.

FLOWER SETS.
MADE IN AMBER, GREEN, ROSE (DAWN), AND AZURE; EXCEPT AS OTHERWISE NOTED.
PRICED PAGE 4—SUPPLEMENTARY PRICE LIST.

Fostoria Glass Company, Moundsville, West Virginia

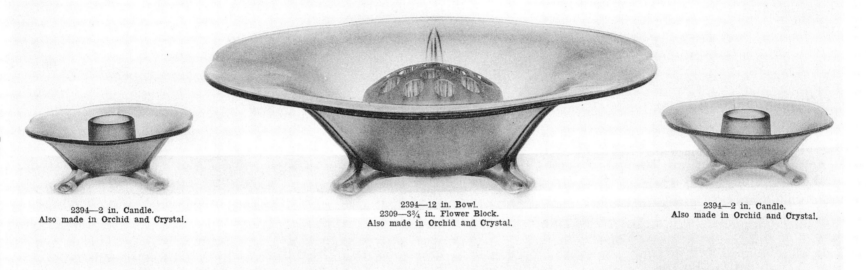

2394—2 in. Candle.
Also made in Orchid and Crystal.

2394—12 in. Bowl.
2309—3¾ in. Flower Block.
Also made in Orchid and Crystal.

2394—2 in. Candle.
Also made in Orchid and Crystal.

2393—2 in. Candle.

2393—12 in. Centerpiece.
Made in 12 and 15 in.
2309—3¾ in. Flower Block.

2393—2 in. Candle.

BOWLS AND CANDLES.
MADE IN AMBER, GREEN, ROSE (DAWN), AZURE AND CRYSTAL; EXCEPT AS OTHERWISE NOTED.
PRICED PAGE 4—SUPPLEMENTARY PRICE LIST.

2383—3 Light Candle (Trindle)

2398—11 in. Bowl (Cornucopia).
Also made in Orchid.

2395—3 in. Candle.
Also made in Ebony.

2395—10 in. Bowl.
Also made in Ebony.

2395—3 in. Candle.
Also made in Ebony.

Fostoria Glass Company, Moundsville, West Virginia

TABLEWARE.
MADE IN AMBER, GREEN, ROSE (DAWN), AZURE, ORCHID AND CRYSTAL; EXCEPT AS OTHERWISE NOTED.
PRICED PAGE 6—SUPPLEMENTARY PRICE LIST.

3

Fostoria Glass Company, Moundsville, West Virginia

2394—4½ in. Mint.

2315—12 in. Salver.

2374—Individual Nut.
Not made in Orchid.

2374—6 in. Nut Bowl.
Not made in Orchid.

2400—8 in. Comport.

2315—Mayonnaise.
2315—13 in. Lettuce Plate.

MISCELLANEOUS GLASSWARE.
MADE IN AMBER, GREEN, ROSE (DAWN), AZURE, ORCHID AND CRYSTAL.
PRICED PAGES 6 & 7—SUPPLEMENTARY PRICE LIST.

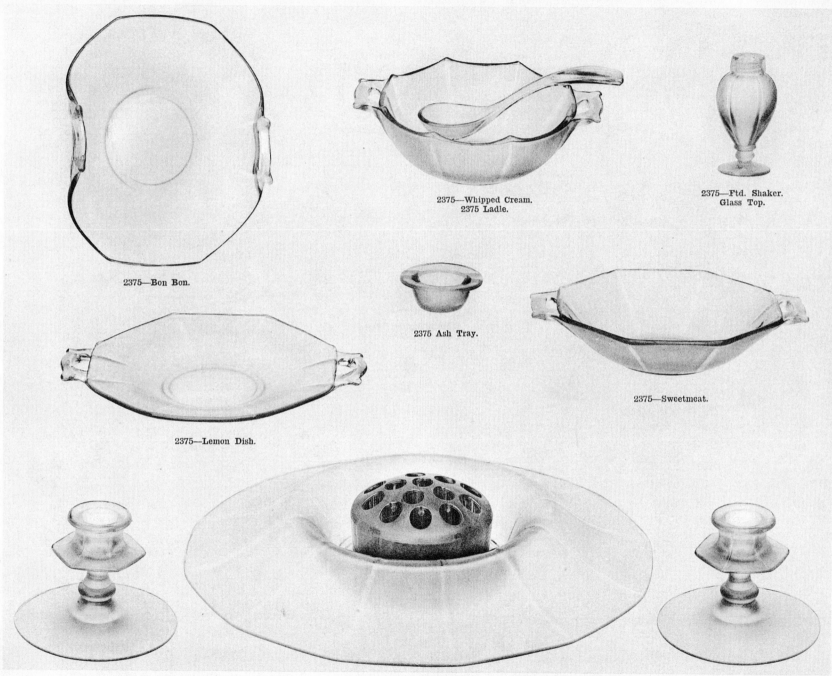

2375—Whipped Cream.
2375 Ladle.

2375—Ftd. Shaker.
Glass Top.

2375—Bon Bon.

2375 Ash Tray.

2375—Sweetmeat.

2375—Lemon Dish.

2375—3 in. Candle.

2375—12 in. Centerpiece.
Made in 12 & 15 in.
15 in. Not made in crystal.
2309—3¾ in. Flower Block.

2375—3 in. Candle.

Fostoria Glass Company, Moundsville, West Virginia

MISCELLANEOUS GLASSWARE.
MADE IN AMBER, GREEN, ROSE (DAWN), AZURE, ORCHID AND CRYSTAL; EXCEPT AS OTHERWISE NOTED.
PRICED PAGES 4 & 6—SUPLEMENTARY PRICE LIST.

Fostoria Glass Company, Moundsville, West Virginia

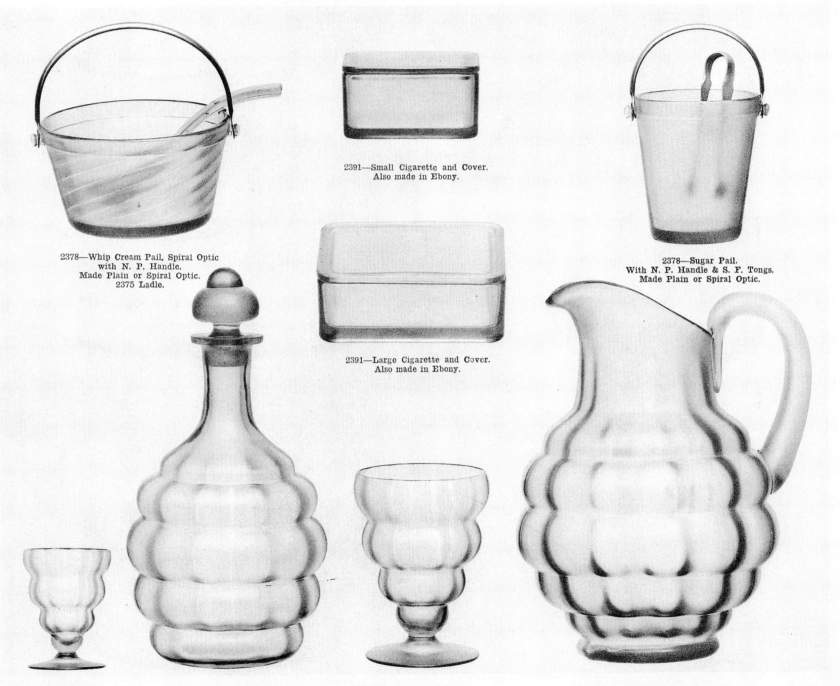

2378—Whip Cream Pail. Spiral Optic
with N. P. Handle.
Made Plain or Spiral Optic.
2375 Ladle.

2391—Small Cigarette and Cover.
Also made in Ebony.

2391—Large Cigarette and Cover.
Also made in Ebony.

2378—Sugar Pail.
With N. P. Handle & S. F. Tongs.
Made Plain or Spiral Optic.

4101—2½ oz.
Ftd. Tumbler.
Not made in Orchid or Crystal.

4101—Quart Decanter.
Not made in Orchid or Crystal.

4101—9 oz. Ftd. Tumbler.
Not made in Orchid or Crystal.

4101—Jug.
Not made in Orchid or Crystal.

VASES.
MADE IN GREEN, ROSE (DAWN) AND AZURE; EXCEPT AS OTHERWISE NOTED.
PRICED PAGE 5—SUPPLEMENTARY PRICE LIST.

2387—8 in. Vase.
Also made in Orchid and Crystal.

2385—8½ in. Fan Vase.
Also made in Ebony,
Orchid and Crystal.

2397—4 in. Vase, Optic.
Made in 4-6 and 8 in.

2397—6 in. Vase, Optic.
Made in 4-6 and 8 in.

2397—8 in. Vase, Optic.
Made in 4-6 and 8 in.

Fostoria Glass Company, Moundsville, West Virginia

VASES.
MADE IN GREEN, ROSE (DAWN), AZURE, ORCHID AND CRYSTAL; EXCEPT AS OTHERWISE NOTED.
PRICED PAGE 5—SUPPLEMENTARY PRICE LIST.

Fostoria Glass Company, Moundsville, West Virginia

2373—Large Window Vase and Cover.
Also made in Ebony.

2373—Small Window Vase and Cover.
Also made in Ebony.

4105—6 in. Vase, Regular Optic.
Made Reg. Opt. in Gr-Ro-Az-Or-Cry.
Made Loop Opt. in Gr-Ro-Az.

4105—8 in. Vase, Regular Optic.
Made Reg. Opt. in Gr-Ro-Az-Or-Cry.
Made Loop Opt. in Gr-Ro-Az.

4105—10 in. Vase, Loop Optic.
Made Reg. Opt. in Gr-Ro-Az.
Made Loop Opt. in Gr-Ro-Az.

No. 2222 TEA ROOM SERVICE.
MADE IN AMBER AND GREEN.
PRICED PAGE 5—SUPPLEMENTARY PRICE LIST.

2222½—Sugar and Cover.

1372—Oyster Cocktail.
1372—Oyster Cocktail Liner.

2222—5 oz. Parfait.

2222—Ind. Cream.
No Handle.

2222—Finger Bowl.
2222—6 in. F. B. Plate.

2222—10 oz. Goblet.

2222—4½ oz. Low Sherbet.

2222—3 oz. Low Sherbet.

2222—3½ oz. Fruit Cocktail.

Fostoria Glass Company, Moundsville, West Virginia

No. 2222 TEA ROOM SERVICE.
MADE IN AMBER AND GREEN.
PRICED PAGE 5—SUPPLEMENTARY PRICE LIST.

Fostoria Glass Company, Moundsville, West Virginia

713½—Shaker.
Glass Top.

2222—4 oz. Oil.
Ground Stopper.

2222—6 oz. Oil.
Ground Stopper.

2222½—Water Bottle.
Capacity 46 ozs.

2222½—14 oz.
Ice Tea Tumbler.

2222½—8 oz.
Table Tumbler.

2222½—5 oz. Tumbler.

5298 BLOWN STEMWARE.
MADE IN AMBER, GREEN, ROSE (DAWN) AND AZURE BOWL WITH CRYSTAL STEM AND FOOT—REGULAR OPTIC.
THIS LINE IN SOLID CRYSTAL IS 5098.
PRICED PAGE 12—SUPPLEMENTARY PRICE LIST.

5298—4 oz. Claret.
Optic.

5298—3½ oz. Cocktail.
Optic.

5298—3 oz. Wine.
Optic.

5298—6 oz. Parfait.
Optic.

5298—¾ oz. Cordial.
Optic.

5298—10 oz. Goblet.
Optic.

5298—6 oz. High Sherbet.
Optic.

5298—6 oz. Low Sherbet.
Optic.

5298—5½ oz. Oyster Cocktail.
Optic.

Fostoria Glass Company, Moundsville, West Virginia

TABLEWARE.
MADE IN AMBER, BLUE, GREEN AND CRYSTAL; EXCEPT AS OTHERWISE NOTED.
PRICED PAGE 8 — No. 2 SUPPLEMENT PRICE LIST.

Fostoria Glass Company, Moundsville, West Virginia

No. 2111—Shaker.
F. G. Top.
Also made in orchid.

No. 2127—Shaker.
F. G. Top.

No. 2128—Shaker.
F. G. Top.

No. 2255—Sugar.

No. 2255—Cream.

No. 5100—Shaker Optic.
F. G. Top.
Also made in orchid.

No. 4095—Salt, optic.
Solid colors or colored foot.

No. 2222—Ftd. Salt.

No. 2321—Sherbet.
No. 2321—8 in. Plate.

No. 2378—Ice Bucket.
With N. P. Handle, Drainer and Tongs.
Also made in orchid.
Patent Applied for.

No. 1913½—Ind. Salt.
No. 2000—Condiment Tray.

No. 2321—Cup.
No. 2321—Saucer.

PLATES.
MADE IN AMBER, BLUE AND GREEN; EXCEPT AS OTHERWISE NOTED.
PRICED PAGE 11 — No. 2 SUPPLEMENT PRICE LIST.

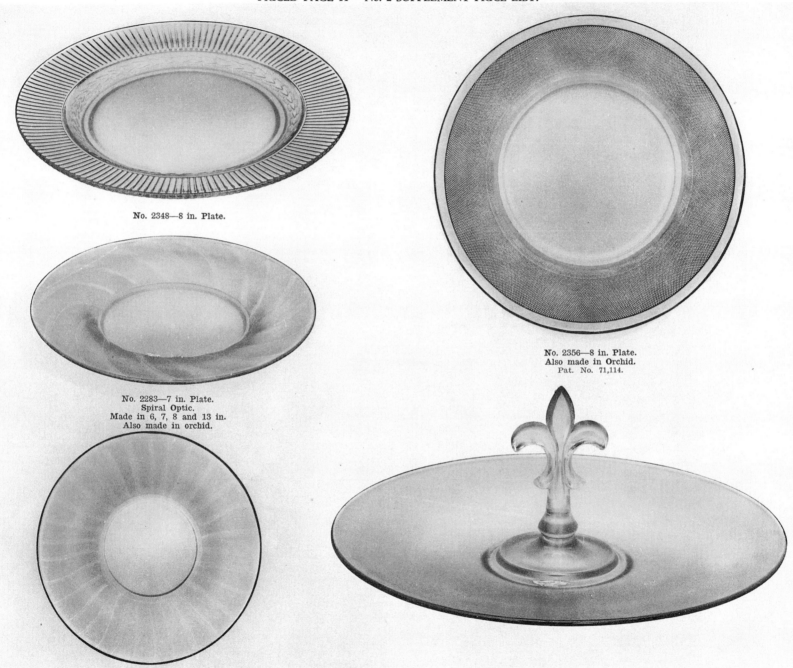

No. 2348—8 in. Plate.

No. 2283—7 in. Plate.
Spiral Optic.
Made in 6, 7, 8 and 13 in.
Also made in orchid.

No. 2356—8 in. Plate.
Also made in Orchid.
Pat. No. 71,114.

No. 2283—6 in. Plate, Reg. Optic.
6, 7 and 8 in. made in Amber, Blue & Green.
6 in. also made in orchid.

No. 2287—11 in. Hld. Sandwich Tray.
Also made in orchid.
Patent No. 65,421.

Fostoria Glass Company, Moundsville, West Virginia

5298 BLOWN LINE AND MISCELLANEOUS WARE.
MADE IN AMBER, GREEN, ROSE (DAWN) AND AZURE BOWL WITH CRYSTAL STEM AND FOOT—REGULAR OPTIC,
EXCEPT AS OTHERWISE NOTED.
THIS LINE IN SOLID CRYSTAL IS 5098.
PRICED PAGE 12—SUPPLEMENTARY PRICE LIST.

13

Fostoria Glass Company, Moundsville, West Virginia

5298—5 in. Comport.
Optic.

5282½—Grape Fruit.
945½—G. F. Liner.
Optic.

869—Finger Bowl.
2283—6 in. F. B. Plate.
Optic.
Made in Solid Colors.

5298—6 in. Nappy.
Optic.

5298—2½ oz.
Ftd. Tumbler.
Optic.

5298—5 oz. Ftd. Tumbler.
Optic.

5298—9 oz. Ftd. Tumbler.
Optic.

5298—12 oz. Ftd. Tumbler.
Optic.

5000—7 Ftd. Jug.
Optic.
Made in Solid Color.

"EILENE" PATTERN, NEEDLE ETCHING No. 83.
MADE IN GREEN, ROSE (DAWN) AND AZURE BOWL WITH CRYSTAL STEM AND FOOT; ALSO MADE SOLID CRYSTAL.
PRICED PAGE 13—SUPPLEMENTARY PRICE LIST.

5282—4½ oz. Claret.
Optic.

5282—2½ oz. Cocktail.
Optic.

5282—2¾ oz. Wine.
Optic.

5282—6 oz. Parfait.
Optic.

5282—¾ oz. Cordial.
Optic.

5282—9 oz. Goblet.
Optic.

5282—5 oz. High Sherbet.
Optic.

5282—5 oz. Low Sherbet.
Optic.

4295—4 oz. Oyster Cocktail.
Optic.

Fostoria Glass Company, Moundsville, West Virginia

"EILENE" PATTERN, NEEDLE ETCHING No. 83.
MADE IN GREEN, ROSE (DAWN) AND AZURE BOWL WITH CRYSTAL STEM AND FOOT, ALSO SOLID CRYSTAL.
PRICED PAGE 13—SUPPLEMENTARY PRICE LIST.

15

Fostoria Glass Company, Moundsville, West Virginia

5282½—Grape Fruit.
945½—G. F. Liner.
Optic.

869—Finger Bowl.
2283—6 in. F. B. Plate.
Optic.

2283—7 inch Plate.

4295—2½ oz. Ftd. Tumbler.
Optic.

4295—5 oz. Ftd. Tumbler.
Optic.

4295—9 oz. Ftd. Tumbler.
Optic.

4295—12 oz. Ftd. Tumbler.
Optic.

4095—7 Ftd. Jug.
Solid Colors.
Optic.

"CAMDEN" PATTERN, NEEDLE ETCHING No. 84.
MADE IN AMBER AND GREEN BOWL WITH CRYSTAL STEM AND FOOT.
PRICED PAGE 13—SUPPLEMENTARY PRICE LIST.

5298—4 oz. Claret.
Optic.

5298—3½ oz. Cocktail.
Optic.

5298—3 oz. Wine.
Optic.

5298—6 oz. Parfait.
Optic.

5298—¾ oz. Cordial.
Optic.

5298—10 oz. Goblet.
Optic.

5298—6 oz. High Sherbet.
Optic.

5298—6 oz. Low Sherbet.
Optic.

5298—5½ oz. Oyster Cocktail.
Optic.

Fostoria Glass Company, Moundsville, West Virginia

"CAMDEN" PATTERN, NEEDLE ETCHING No. 84.
MADE IN AMBER AND GREEN; BOWL WITH CRYSTAL STEM AND FOOT.
PRICED PAGE 13—SUPPLEMENTARY PRICE LIST.

17

Fostoria Glass Company, Moundsville, West Virginia

5298—5 in. Comport.
Optic.

5282½—Grape Fruit.
945½—G. F. Liner.
Optic.

5298—6 in. Nappy.
Optic.

869—Finger Bowl.
2283—6 in. F. B. Plate.
Optic.

5298—2½ oz. Ftd. Tumbler.
Optic.

5298—5 oz. Ftd. Tumbler.
Optic.

5298—9 oz. Ftd. Tumbler.
Optic.

5298—12 oz. Ftd. Tumbler.
Optic.

5000—7 Ftd. Jug.
Optic.
Solid Color.

"VERSAILLES" PATTERN, PLATE ETCHING No. 278.
MADE IN GREEN, ROSE (DAWN) AND AZURE BOWL WITH CRYSTAL STEM AND FOOT.
PRICED PAGES 14 AND 15—SUPPLEMENTARY PRICE LIST.

5298—10 oz. Goblet.
Optic.

5298—6 oz. High Sherbet.
Optic.

5298—6 oz. Low Sherbet.
Optic.

5298—5½ oz. Oyster Cocktail.
Optic.

5298—5 oz. Ftd. Tumbler.
Optic.

5298—9 oz. Ftd. Tumbler.
Optic.

5298—12 oz. Ftd. Tumbler.
Optic.

5000—7 Ftd. Jug.
Optic.
Made in Solid Color.

Fostoria Glass Company, Moundsville, West Virginia

"VERSAILLES" PATTERN, PLATE ETCHING No. 278.
MADE IN GREEN, ROSE (DAWN) AND AZURE.
PRICED PAGES 14 AND 15—SUPPLEMENTARY PRICE LIST.

19

Fostoria Glass Company, Moundsville, West Virginia

2375—7 in. Comport.

2375—11 in. Hld. Lunch Tray.

2375—7 in. Salad Plate.

2375—8½ in. Relish.

2375—9 in. Baker.

2375—9 in. Dinner Plate.

"VERSAILLES" PATTERN, PLATE ETCHING No. 278.
MADE IN GREEN, ROSE (DAWN) AND AZURE.
PRICED PAGES 14 AND 15—SUPPLEMENTARY PRICE LIST.

2375—Ftd. Cream Soup.
2375—Cream Soup Plate.

2375—Ftd. Bouillon.
2375—Saucer.

2375—Ftd. Shaker.
with glass top.

2375½—Ftd. Sugar & Cover.

2375½—Ftd. Cream.

2375½—Ftd. Cup.
2375—Saucer.

2375—6 in. Cereal.

2375—After Dinner Cup.
2375—A. D. Saucer.

2375—Ftd. Mayonnaise.
2375—Mayonnaise Plate.
2375—Mayonnaise Ladle.

Fostoria Glass Company, Moundsville, West Virginia

"VERSAILLES" PATTERN, PLATE ETCHING No. 278.
MADE IN GREEN, ROSE (DAWN) AND AZURE.
PRICED PAGES 14 AND 15—SUPPLEMENTARY PRICE LIST.

21

Fostoria Glass Company, Moundsville, West Virginia

2331—3 Candy Box & Cover.

2375—Sweetmeat.

2375—Bon Bon.

2375—Lemon Dish.

2375—Whipped Cream.
2375—Ladle.

2378—Sugar Pail.
With N. P. Handle
& S. F. Tongs.

2378—Whip Cream Pail.
With N. P. Handle.
2375—Ladle.

2378—Ice Bucket.
With N. P. Handle,
Drainer & Tongs.

"JUNE" PATTERN, PLATE ETCHING No. 279.
MADE IN ROSE (DAWN) AND AZURE; EXCEPT AS OTHERWISE NOTED.
PRICED PAGES 15-16 AND 17—SUPPLEMENTARY PRICE LIST.

2375—Bon Bon.

2375—Sweetmeat.

2375—Ftd. Bouillon.
2375—Saucer.

2375—Lemon Dish.

2375—6 in. Cereal.

2375—Whipped Cream.
2375—Ladle.

2375½—Ftd. Sugar & Cover.
Also made in Crystal.

2375½—Ftd. Cream.
Also made in Crystal.

2368—Ftd. Cheese.
2368—11 in. Cracker Plate.

2375—Ftd. Cream Soup.
2375—7 in. Cream Soup Plate.

Fostoria Glass Company, Moundsville, West Virginia

"JUNE" PATTERN, PLATE ETCHING No. 279.
MADE IN ROSE (DAWN) AND AZURE; EXCEPT AS OTHERWISE NOTED.
PRICED PAGES 15-16 AND 17—SUPPLEMENTARY PRICE LIST.

Fostoria Glass Company, Moundsville, West Virginia

2375—8 in. Salad Plate.
Also made in Crystal.

2375—After Dinner Cup.
2375—A. D. Saucer.

2375—Ftd. Shaker.
Glass Top.
Also made in Crystal.

2375—8½ in. Relish.

2375½—Ftd. Cup.
2375—Saucer.

2375—5 in. Fruit.

2375—9 in. Baker.

2375—12 in. Platter.

2375—Ftd. Mayonnaise.
2375—7 in. Mayonnaise Plate.
2375—Mayonnaise Ladle.

"JUNE" PATTERN, PLATE ETCHING No. 279.
MADE IN ROSE (DAWN), AND AZURE. BOWL WITH CRYSTAL STEM AND FOOT, ALSO SOLID CRYSTAL.
PRICED PAGES 15-16 AND 17—SUPPLEMENTARY PRICE LIST.

5298—10 oz. Goblet.
Optic.

5298—6 oz. High Sherbet.
Optic.

5298—6 oz. Low Sherbet.
Optic.

5298—5½ oz. Oyster Cocktail.
Optic.

5298—5 oz. Ftd. Tumbler.
Optic.

5298—9 oz. Ftd. Tumbler.
Optic.

5298—12 oz. Ftd. Tumbler.
Optic.

5000—7 Ftd. Jug.
Optic.
Made in Solid Color.

Fostoria Glass Company, Moundsville, West Virginia

Fostoria Glass Company, Moundsville, West Virginia

2394—2 in. Candle.

2394—12 in. Bowl.
2309—3¾ in. Flower Block.

2394—2 in. Candle.

2395—3 in. Candle.

2395—10 in. Bowl.

2395—3 in. Candle.

"OAK LEAF" PATTERN, BROCADE PLATE ETCHING No. 290.
MADE IN GREEN AND CRYSTAL.
PRICED PAGES 17 AND 18—SUPPLEMENTARY PRICE LIST.

877—10 oz. Goblet.
Optic.

877—6 oz. High Sherbet.
Optic.

877—6 oz. Low Sherbet.
Optic.

877—4½ oz. Oyster Cocktail.
Optic.

877—5 oz. Ftd. Tumbler.
Optic.

877—9 oz. Ftd. Tumbler.
Optic.

877—12 oz. Ftd. Tumbler.
Optic.

5000—7 Ftd. Jug.
Optic.

Fostoria Glass Company, Moundsville, West Virginia

"OAK LEAF" PATTERN, BROCADE PLATE ETCHING No. 290.
MADE IN GREEN, ROSE (DAWN) AND CRYSTAL; EXCEPT AS OTHERWISE NOTED.
PRICED PAGES 17 AND 18—SUPPLEMENTARY PRICE LIST.

Fostoria Glass Company, Moundsville, West Virginia

2378—Whip Cream Pail.
With N. P. Handle.
2375—Ladle.

2378—Sugar Pail.
With N. P. Handles
& S F. Tongs.

2380—Confection & Cover.

2375—Bon Bon.

2391—Small Cigarette & Cover.
Also made in Ebony.

2391—Large Cigarette & Cover.
Also made in Ebony.

2394—2 in. Candle.

2394—12 in. Bowl.
2309—3¾ in. Flower Block.

2394—2 in. Candle.

"OAK LEAF" PATTERN, BROCADE PLATE ETCHING No. 290.
MADE IN GREEN, ROSE (DAWN) AND CRYSTAL; EXCEPT AS OTHERWISE NOTED.
PRICED PAGES 17 AND 18—SUPPLEMENTARY PRICE LIST.

2398—11 in. Bowl.

2394—4½ in. Mint.

2400—8 in. Comport.

2395—3 in. Candle.
Also made in Ebony.

2395—10 in. Bowl.
Also made in Ebony.

2395—3 in. Candle.
Also made in Ebony.

Fostoria Glass Company, Moundsville, West Virginia

"OAK LEAF" PATTERN, BROCADE PLATE ETCHING No. 290.
MADE IN GREEN, ROSE (DAWN) AND CRYSTAL; EXCEPT AS OTHERWISE NOTED.
PRICED PAGES 17 AND 18—SUPPLEMENTARY PRICE LIST.

2369—7 in. Vase.
Optic.

2373—Small Window Vase & Cover.
Also made in Ebony.

4103—3 in. Vase.
Optic.

4105—8 in. Vase.
Optic.

2385—8½ in. Fan Vase.
Also made in Ebony.

2387—8 in. Vase.

Fostoria Glass Company, Moundsville, West Virginia

"THELMA" PATTERN, CUTTING No. 186.
MADE IN AMBER, GREEN, ROSE (DAWN) AND ORCHID.
PRICED PAGE 19—SUPPLEMENTARY PRICE LIST.

2369—7 in. Vase.
Optic.

4100—8 in. Vase.
Optic.

4103—5 in. Vase.
Optic.

2362—3 in. Candle.

2362—12 in. Bowl.
2309—3¾ in. Flower Block.

2362—3 in. Candle.

Fostoria Glass Company, Moundsville, West Virginia

"THELMA" PATTERN, CUTTING No. 186.
MADE IN AMBER, GREEN, ROSE (DAWN) AND ORCHID.
PRICED PAGE 19—SUPPLEMENTARY PRICE LIST.

Fostoria Glass Company, Moundsville, West Virginia

2342—12 in. Hld. Lunch Tray.

2331—3 Candy Box & Cover.

2297—12 in. Deep Bowl "A."

2327—7 in. Comport.

2342—12 in. Deep Bowl "A."

"BERRY" PATTERN, CUTTING No. 188.
MADE IN GREEN AND ROSE (DAWN) BOWL WITH CRYSTAL STEM AND FOOT.
PRICED PAGE 20— SUPPLEMENTARY PRICE LIST.

5298—5½ oz. Oyster Cocktail.
Optic.

5298—10 oz. Goblet.
Optic.

5298—6 oz. High Sherbet.
Optic.

5298—6 oz. Low Sherbet.
Optic.

5298—5 oz. Ftd. Tumbler.
Optic.

5298—9 oz. Ftd. Tumbler.
Optic.

5298—12 oz. Ftd. Tumbler.
Optic.

5000—7 Ftd. Jug.
Optic.
Made in Solid Color.

Fostoria Glass Company, Moundsville, West Virginia

"BERRY" PATTERN, CUTTING No. 188.
MADE IN GREEN AND ROSE (DAWN).
PRICED PAGE 20— SUPPLEMENTARY PRICE LIST.

Fostoria Glass Company, Moundsville, West Virginia

2350½—Ftd. Sugar.

2350½—Ftd. Cream.

2394—4½ in. Mint.

2400—8 in. Comport.

2378—Ice Bucket.
With N. P. Handle, Drainer & Tongs.

2378—Whip Cream Pail.
With N. P. Handle.
2375—Ladle.

2378—Sugar Pail.
With N. P. Handle
& S. F. Tongs.

"BERRY" PATTERN, CUTTING No. 188.
MADE IN GREEN AND ROSE (DAWN).
PRICED PAGE 20— SUPPLEMENTARY PRICE LIST.

2394—2 in. Candle.

2394—12 in. Bowl.
2309—3¾ in. Flower Block.

2394—2 in. Candle.

2315—Mayonnaise.
2315—13 in. Lettuce Plate.
2375—Mayonnaise Ladle.

2331—3 Candy Box & Cover.

2324—4 in. Candle.

2329—11 in. Centerpiece.
2309—3¾ in. Flower Block.

2324—4 in. Candle.

Fostoria Glass Company, Moundsville, West Virginia

"BERRY" PATTERN, CUTTING No. 188.
MADE IN GREEN AND ROSE (DAWN).
PRICED PAGE 20— SUPPLEMENTARY PRICE LIST.

35

Fostoria Glass Company, Moundsville, West Virginia

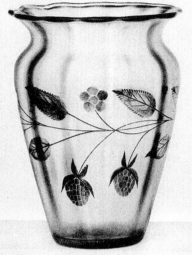

4105—6 in. Vase.
Optic.

2373—Large Window Vase & Cover.

4105—8 in. Vase.
Optic.

4100—8 in. Vase.
Optic.

4103—6 in. Vase.
Optic.

2369—7 in. Vase.
Optic.

MISCELLANEOUS CUT WARE.
MADE IN GREEN, ROSE (DAWN) AND AZURE.
PRICED PAGE 19—SUPPLEMENTARY PRICE LIST.

2375—Sweetmeat.
Cut A.

2385—8½ in. Fan Vase.
Cut B.

2375—Bon Bon.
Cut C.

2391—Small Cigarette.
Cut A.

2391—Large Cigarette.
Cut C.

2385—8½ in. Fan Vase.
Cut A.

2375—Lemon Dish.
Cut B.

2385—8½ in. Fan Vase.
Cut C.

Fostoria Glass Company, Moundsville, West Virginia

"GRAPE" PATTERN, PLATE ETCHING No. 287.
MADE IN BLUE, GREEN AND ORCHID.
PRICED PAGE 36 — No. 2 SUPPLEMENT PRICE LIST.

37

Fostoria Glass Company, Moundsville, West Virginia

2292—8 in. Vase.

4100—6 in. Vase.
Optic.

4103—5 in. Vase.
Optic.

2372—2 in. Candle.

2371—13 in. Centerpiece (Oval).
2371—Flower Holder.

2372—2 in. Candle.

"CUPID" PATTERN, PLATE ETCHING No. 288.
MADE IN BLUE, GREEN AND EBONY.
PRICED PAGE 36 — No. 2 SUPPLEMENT PRICE LIST.

2322—Cologne.

2359½—Puff and Cover.

2322—Cologne.

2276—Vanity Set.

2298—Candle.

2298—Clock.

2298—Candle.

Fostoria Glass Company, Moundsville, West Virginia

PLATE ETCHED CIGARETTE HOLDERS.
MADE IN SOLID AMBER, BLUE, GREEN, EBONY AND CRYSTAL.
PRICED PAGE 35 — No. 2 SUPPLEMENT PRICE LIST.

39

Fostoria Glass Company, Moundsville, West Virginia

2354—Cigarette.
Etched Dog.

2354—Cigarette.
Etched Horse.

2354—Cigarette.
Etched Cupid.

2354—Cigarette.
Etched Deer.

2324—4 in. Candle.

2329—11 in. Centerpiece.
2309—3¾ in Flower Block.

2324—4 in. Candle.

"ROYAL" PATTERN, PLATE ETCHING No. 273.
MADE IN AMBER, BLUE, GREEN AND CRYSTAL.
PRICED PAGES 28 AND 29 — No. 2 SUPPLEMENT PRICE LIST.
Design Patent Nos. 68,424 and 68,425.

869—9 oz. Goblet.
Optic.

869—6 oz. Parfait.
Optic.

869—5½ oz High Sherbet.
Optic.

869—5½ oz. Low Sherbet.
Optic.

5100—Ftd. Shaker.
Optic. F. G. Top.

869—Finger Bowl.
2283—6 in. Finger Bowl Plate.
Optic.

5100—9 oz.
Ftd. Tumbler.
Optic.

5100—5 oz.
Ftd. Tumbler.
Optic.

5100—2½ oz.
Ftd. Tumbler.
Optic.

869—Table Tumbler.
Optic.

1236—No. 6 Jug.
Optic.

Fostoria Glass Company, Moundsville, West Virginia

Fostoria

Fine Crystal and Colored Glassware
Cut, Etched and Plain

REPRINT OF A CATALOG
1925-1930

© 2000

L-W BOOK SALES
PO Box 69
Gas City, IN 46933

Fostoria Glass Company, Moundsville, West Virginia.

No. 660-¾ oz. Cordial.

No. 660-3oz. Cocktail.

No. 660-2½ oz. Wine.

No. 660-5 oz. Parfait

No. 837. Oyster Cocktail.

No. 660-5 oz. Fruit.

No. 660-5 oz. Saucer Champagne.

No. 660-9 oz. Goblet.

No. 887–2½ oz. Tumbler.   No. 889–5 oz. Tumbler.   No. 4095–5 oz. Tumbler, Footed.   No. 4095–13 oz. Tumbler, Footed.

No. 889–8 oz. Tumbler.   No. 4076–9 oz. Tumbler   No. 889–13 oz. Tumbler.   No. 4011–12 oz. Tumbler, Handled.

Fostoria Glass Company, Moundsville, West Virginia.

Fostoria Glass Company, Moundsville, West Virginia.

No. 661-¾ oz. Cordial.　　No. 661-2½ oz. Cocktail.　　No. 661-2oz. Wine.　　No. 661-5½ oz. Parfait.

No. 837. Oyster Cocktail.　　No. 661-6 oz. Fruit.　　No. 661-6 oz. Saucer Champagne.　　No. 661-9 oz. Goblet.

"Airdale" Pattern.   Cutting No. 175

No. 803 – 5 in. Nappy   No. 820 Table Tumbler   No. 701 – 13 oz. Tumbler   No. 880 – Bon Bon

No. 1769 Finger Bowl
No. 2283 – 6 in. Plate

No. 880. 5½ oz. Fruit.   No. 880. 5½ oz. Saucer Champagne.   No. 880. 10 oz. Goblet.   No. 2040/3. Jug.

Fostoria Glass Company, Moundsville, West Virginia.

Fostoria Glass Company, Moundsville, West Virginia.

No. 2263 Ind. Salt, Eng. 26.

No. 880 Ftd. Salt, Eng. 26.

No. 2272 Coaster Cut 172.

No. 1590—3½ in. Coaster Cut 171.

No. 803—7 in. Nappy.

No. 2276. Vanity Set, Eng. A.

No. 2219—½ lb. Candy Jar and Cover.

No. 1852-6 Jug.

Blown Bud Vases, Etched and Cut.

Fostoria Glass Company, Moundsville, West Virginia.

No. 4069-9 in. Vase.
Eng. 25

No. 765-10 in. Vase.
Cut 173

No. 765-10 in. Vase.
Et. A.

No. 765-10 in. Vase.
Eng. 27

No. 765-10 in. Vase.
Et. A.

Fostoria Glass Company, Moundsville, West Virginia

No. 1432 Sugar Cut E

No. 1432 Cream Cut E

No. 5085-8 in. Bud Vase.
Cut 31

No. 5086-9 in. Bud Vase.
Cut 32

No. 765-10 in. Bud Vase
Cut 80

No. 5087-8 in. Bud Vase.
Cut 83

No. 762-8 in Vase
Cut 181

Miscellaneous Cut Ware.

No. 2315 Bowl B Shape Cut D

Fostoria Glass Company, Moundsville, West Virginia

No. 4055-D. Vase, Cut 182   No. 2072-8 in. Vase, Cut 182   No. 4095½-8 in. Vase, Cut 182   No. 4069-9 in. Vase, Cut 181

Fostoria Glass Company, Moundsville, West Virginia

No. 2276 Covered Cheese Cut C
No. 2276 Cheese Plate Cut C

No. 2276. Vanity Set.
Cut 15

No. 2331. Candy Box and Cover.
Cut D

No. 2273. Vanity Set.
Cut 16

No. 701–13 oz. Tumbler

No. 820 Table Tumbler

No. 5082–3 oz. Cocktail

No. 5082–2¾ oz. Wine

No. 5082–6 oz. Parfait

No. 887–2½ oz. Tumbler

No. 1769. Finger Bowl.
No. 1499–6 in. Plate.

No. 5082–5 oz. Fruit.

No. 5082–5 oz. Saucer Champagne.

No. 5082–9 in. Goblet.

Fostoria Glass Company, Moundsville, West Virginia

Fostoria Glass Company, Moundsville, West Virginia

No. 1769 Finger Bowl
No. 2283-6 in. Plate

No. 2315 Sugar

No. 2315 Cream

No. 2315 Mayonnaise Set

No. 4011-12 oz. Hld. Tumbler.   No. 5083-5½ oz. Fruit.   No. 5083-5½ oz. Saucer Champagne   No. 5983-9 oz. Goblet.

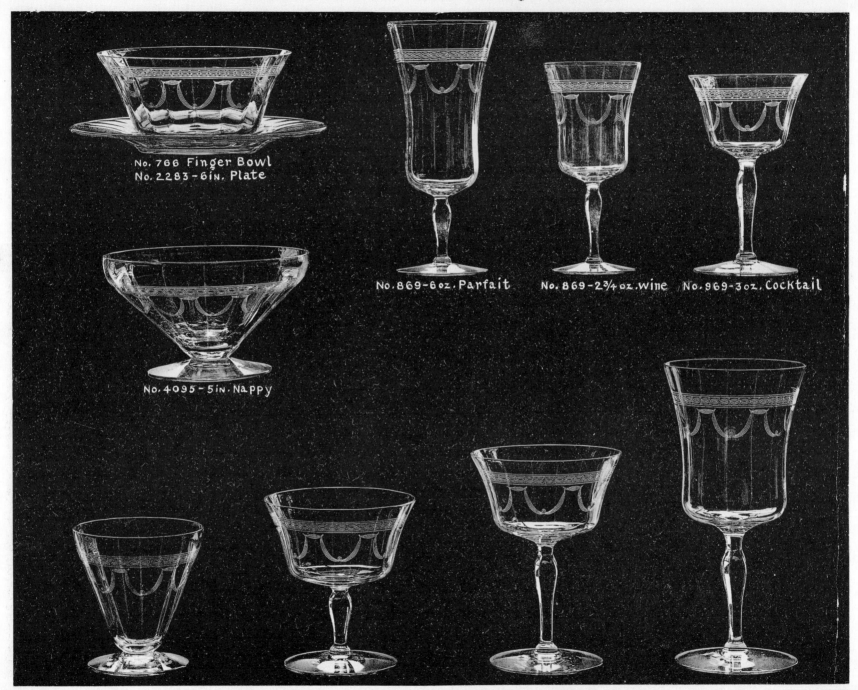

No. 766 Finger Bowl
No. 2283-6in. Plate

No. 869-6oz. Parfait

No. 869-2¾oz. Wine

No. 969-3oz. Cocktail

No. 4095-5in. Nappy

No. 4095. Oyster Cocktail.

No. 869-5½ oz. Fruit.

No. 869-5½ oz. Saucer Champagne.

No. 869-9 oz. Goblet.

Fostoria Glass Company, Moundsville, West Virginia

Fostoria Glass Company, Moundsville, West Virginia

No. 869 – 12 oz. Hld Tumbler   No. 869 Table Tumbler   No. 4095 – 2½ oz. Tumbler

No. 4095 – 5 oz. Tumbler.   No. 4095 – 10 oz. Tumbler.   No. 4095 – 13 oz. Tumbler.   No. 4095 – No. 7 Jug.

No. 4095–10 oz. Tumbler   No. 867½–5½ oz. Fruit   No. 867½–5½ oz. Saucer Champagne   No. 867½–9 oz. Goblet

No. 820.   Table Tumbler.   No. 701–13 oz. Tumbler.   No. 316.   No. 7 Jug.

Fostoria Glass Company, Moundsville, West Virginia

Fostoria Glass Company, Moundsville, West Virginia.

No.858-1oz. Cordial.   No. 858-3½oz. Cocktail.   No.858-2¾oz. Wine.   No.858½-5½oz.Parfait.

No. 858.   Oyster Cocktail.   No. 858-5½ oz. Fruit.   No. 858-5½ oz. Saucer Champagne.   No. 858-4½ oz. Claret.   No. 858-9 oz. Goblet.

No.858-3oz. Tumbler.   No.858-5½oz.Tumbler.   No.820-9oz. Table Tumbler.   No.858   Table Tumbler.

No. 858-8 oz. Tumbler.   No. 858-12 oz. Tumbler.   No. 701-12 oz. Ice Tea Tumbler.   No. 4011-12 oz. Tumbler, Handled.   No. 853-14 oz. Ice Tea Tumbler.

Fostoria Glass Company, Moundsville, West Virginia.

Fostoria Glass Company, Moundsville, West Virginia.

No. 2283-5 in. Sherbet Plate.

No. 858 Finger Bowl.
No. 2283-6 in. Finger Bowl Plate.

No. 858-3 Piece Mayonnaise Set.   No. 858. Sweetmeat.   No. 880. Bon Bon.

No. 2133 Sugar.

No. 2133 Cream.

No. 312. Oil.

No. 945½. Grape Fruit and Liner.

No. 300-No. 7 Jug.

Fostoria Glass Company, Moundsville, West Virginia.

Fostoria Glass Company, Moundsville, West Virginia.

No.5082–¾ oz. Cordial.   No.5082–3oz. Cocktail   No.5082–2¾ oz.Wine   No.5082–6 oz.Parfait   No.5082–4½ oz. Claret

No.1769– Finger Bowl
No.2283–6 in. Plate

No. 837. Oyster Cocktail.   No. 5082. 5 oz. Fruit.   No. 5082. 5 oz. Saucer Champagne.   No. 5082. 9 oz. Goblet.

NO-4095-2½ oz. Footed Tumbler   No. 4095-5 oz. Footed Tumbler.   No. 4095-10 oz. Footed Tumbler.   No. 4095-13 oz. Footed Tumbler

No. 887
2½ oz. Tumbler.

No. 889
5 oz. Tumbler.

No. 820
Table Tumbler.

No. 701
8 oz. Tumbler.

No. 701
13 oz. Tumbler.

No. 837
12 oz. Tumbler, Handled.

Fostoria Glass Company, Moundsville, West Virginia.

No. 2283 – 7 in. Plate

No. 945 ½ Grape Fruit
No. 945 ½ Grape Fruit Liner

No. 858 Sweet Meat

No. 5078. 5 in. Nappy.

No. 5078. 6 in. Nappy.

No. 5078. 5 in. Comport.

NO. 2270 NO. 7. Jug and Cover

No. 303. No. 7 Jug.

No. 318. No. 7 Jug.

Fostoria Glass Company, Moundsville, West Virginia.

PATENT No. 63,930

Fostoria Glass Company, Moundsville, West Virginia

No. 5078-7 in. Nappy.

No. 766 Bon Bon.

No. 5078-6 in. Comport.

No. 5078-5 in. Nappy and Cover.

No. 825. Jelly and Cover.

No. 5078-5 in. Comport and Cover.

"Washington" Pattern Plate Etching 266
PATENT No. 63,930

No. 660–¾ oz. Cordial.   No. 660–3 oz. Cocktail.   No. 660–2½ oz. Wine.   No. 660–5 oz. Parfait.   No. 660–4 oz. Claret.

No. 837. Oyster Cocktail.   No. 660. 5 oz. Fruit.   No. 660. 5 oz. Saucer Champagne.   No. 660. 9 oz. Goblet.

Fostoria Glass Company, Moundsville, West Virginia

Fostoria Glass Company, Moundsville, West Virginia

No. 4095-2½ oz. Footed Tumbler.　No. 4095-5 oz. Footed Tumbler.　No. 4095-10 oz. Footed Tumbler.　No. 4095-13 oz. Footed Tumbler.

| No. 887 2½ oz. Tumbler. | No. 889 5 oz. Tumbler. | No. 889 8 oz. Tumbler. | No. 4076 9 oz. Table Tumbler. | No. 889 13 oz. Ice Tea Tumbler. | No. 869 12 oz. Tumbler, Handled |

"Washington" Pattern Plate Etching 266
PATENT No. 63,930

No. 2235 Shaker, Pearl Top.   No. 1831 Mustard and Cover.   No. 1851 Sugar.   No. 1851 Cream.

No. 4089. Marmalade and Cover.   No. 2194-8 oz. Syrup, N. T   No. 1465-7 oz. Oil, C/N.   No. 2083. Salad Dressing Bottle.

Fostoria Glass Company, Moundsville, West Virginia

Fostoria Glass Company, Moundsville, West Virginia

No. 2270–No. 7 Jug and Cover.

No. 303–No. 7 Jug.

No. 318–No. 7 Jug.

"Virginia" Pattern Plate Etch 267
PATENT No. 63,929

No. 661–¾ oz. Cordial.   No. 661–2 oz. Wine.   No. 661–3 oz. Cocktail.   No. 661–5½ oz. Parfait.

No. 837. Oyster Cocktail.   No. 661–6 oz. Fruit.   No. 661–6 oz. Saucer Champagne.   No. 661–5½ oz. Claret.   No. 661–9 oz. Goblet.

Fostoria Glass Company, Moundsville, West Virginia

PATENT No. 63,929

Fostoria Glass Company, Moundsville, West Virginia

NO.4095 –2½ oz. Tumbler, Footed.   NO.4095 –5 oz. Tumbler, Footed.   No.4095 –10 oz. Tumbler, Footed.   No.4095 –13 oz. Tumbler, Footed.

| No. 4085 | No. 4085 | No. 4085 | No. 4085 | No. 4085 | No. 869 |
| 2½ oz. Tumbler. | 6 oz. Tumbler. | Table Tumbler. | 13 oz. Tumbler. | 13 oz. Tumbler, Handled. | 12 oz. Tumbler, Handled. |

"Virginia" Pattern Plate Etch 267
PATENT No. 63,929

No. 5078–5 in. Nappy.　　　No. 5078–7 in. Nappy.　　　No. 5078–6 in. Comport.

No. 825. Jelly and Cover.　　　No. 5078-6 in. Nappy and Cover.　　　No. 5078-5 in. Comport and Cover.

Fostoria Glass Company, Moundsville, West Virginia

PATENT No. 63,929

No. 945½ Grape Fruit

No. 945½ Grape Fruit Liner.

No. 1769 Finger Bowl.

No. 1736–6in. Finger Bowl Plate.

Fostoria Glass Company, Moundsville, West Virginia

No. 2138. 3 Piece Mayonnaise Set.

No. 1697. 2 Piece Bed Room Set.

No. 300. Quart Decanter, C/N.

"Virginia" Pattern Plate Etch 267
PATENT No. 63,929

No. 2250–½ Lb. Candy Jar and Cover.

No. 2250–¼ Lb. Candy Jar and Cover.

No. 880. Bon Bon.

No. 303-3. Jug.

No. 1852-6. Jug.

Fostoria Glass Company, Moundsville, West Virginia

Fostoria Glass Company, Moundsville, West Virginia.

No. 2283–5 in. Plate.

No. 2283–7 in. Plate.

No. 2283-8 in. Plate.

No. 1848-9 in. Plate, Matt Star.

No. 661 - 3/4 oz. Cordial   No. 661 - 2 oz. Wine   No. 661 - 3 oz. Cocktail   No. 661 - 5½ oz. Parfait

No. 1769 - Finger Bowl
No. 2283 - 6 in. Plate

No. 837. Oyster Cocktail.   No. 661. 6 oz. Fruit.   No. 661. 6 oz. Saucer Champagne.   No. 661. 5½ oz. Claret.   No. 661. 9 oz. Goblet.

Fostoria Glass Company, Moundsville, West Virginia.

Fostoria Glass Company, Moundsville, West Virginia.

No. 2235
Shaker F.G.T.

No. 4095
2¼ oz. Footed Tumbler.

No. 4095
5 oz. Footed Tumbler.

No. 4095
10 oz. Footed Tumbler.

No. 4095
13 oz. Footed Tumbler.

No. 4085
2½ oz. Tumbler.

No. 4085
6 oz. Tumbler

No. 4085
Table Tumbler.

No. 4085
13 oz. Tumbler.

No. 4085
13 oz. Tumbler, Handled.

No. 2283 - 7 in. Plate

No. 5039 - Oyster Cocktail
No. 5039 - Oyster Cocktail Liner

NO. 2138 - 3 Piece Mayonnaise Set

No. 803. 5 in. Nappy.

No. 803. 5 in. Comport.

No. 825. Jelly and Cover.

Fostoria Glass Company, Moundsville, West Virginia.

Fostoria Glass Company, Moundsville, West Virginia.

No. 4087 – Marmalade and Cover

No. 1480 – Sugar

No. 1480 – Cream

No. 1852.   No. 6 Jug.

No. 1697.   2 Piece Bed Room Set.

No. 4095.   No. 4 Footed Jug.

No. 5082 - ¾ oz. Cordial   No. 5082 - 3 oz. Cocktail   No. 5082 - 2¾ oz. Wine   No. 5082 - 6 oz. Parfait   No. 5082 - 4½ oz. Claret

No. 766 Finger Bowl
No. 2283 - 6 in. Plate

No. 837. Oyster Cocktail.   No. 5082. 5 oz. Fruit.   No. 5082. 5oz. Saucer Champagne.   No. 5082. 9 oz. Goblet.

Fostoria Glass Company, Moundsville, West Virginia.

Fostoria Glass Company, Moundsville, West Virginia.

No. 4095-Footed Almond. No. 4095-2½ oz. Footed Tumbler. No. 4095-5 oz. Footed Tumbler. No. 4095-10 oz. Footed Tumbler.   No. 4095-13 oz. Footed Tumbler

No. 889
2½ oz. Tumbler.

No. 889
5 oz. Tumbler.

No. 4076
Table Tumbler.

No. 889
8 oz. Tumbler.

No. 889
13 oz. Tumbler.

No. 837
12 oz. Tumbler, Handled.

No. 2283 – 7 in. Plate

No. 945½ Grape Fruit
No. 945 ½ Grape Fruit Liner

No. 2138 – 3 Piece Mayonnaise Set

No. 5078. 5 in. Nappy.

No. 5078. 5 in. Comport.

No. 825. Jelly and Cover.

Fostoria Glass Company, Moundsville, West Virginia.

No. 1465 – 5 oz. Oil. Cut Neck.   No. 1968 – Marmalade and Cover

No. 1851 – Sugar

No. 1851 – Cream

No. 318.   No. 7 Jug.

No. 1697.   2 Piece Bed Room Set.

No. 4095.   No. 7 Footed Jug.

No. 660-3/4 oz. Cordial   No. 660-3 oz. Cocktail   No. 660-2½ oz. Wine   No. 660-5 oz. Parfait   660-4 oz. Claret

No. 837. Oyster Cocktail.   No. 660. 5 oz. Fruit.   No. 660. 5 oz. Saucer Champagne.   No. 660. 9 oz. Goblet.

Fostoria Glass Company, Moundsville, West Virginia.

Fostoria Glass Company, Moundsville, West Virginia.

NO. 4095
2 ½ oz. Footed Tumbler

NO. 4095
5 oz. Footed Tumbler

No. 4095 Medium Vase,
Rolled Edge.

No. 4095. 10 oz. Footed Tumbler.

No. 4095. 13 oz. Footed Tumbler.

No. 4095. No. 7 Footed Jug.

Candlesticks Deep Etched.

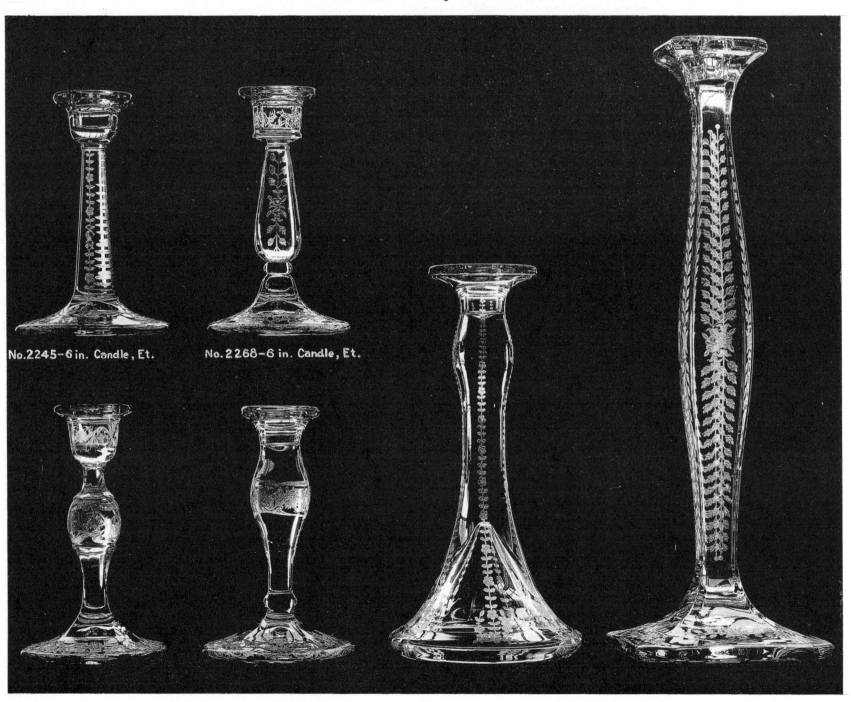

No. 2245-6 in. Candle, Et.

No. 2268-6 in. Candle, Et.

No. 2244-6 in. Candle, Et.

No. 2269-6 in. Candle, Et.

No. 2275-9½ in. Candle, Et.

No. 1490-15 in. Candle, Et.

Fostoria Glass Company, Moundsville, West Virginia.

Fostoria Glass Company, Moundsville, West Virginia

No. 4095-6in. Nappy and Cover

No. 5082-6oz. Parfait

No. 5082-2¾oz. Wine

No. 5082-3oz. Cocktail

No. 4095 Finger Bowl
No. 2283-6in. Plate

No. 4095. Oyster Cocktail.

No. 5082-5 oz. Fruit.

No. 5082-5 oz. Saucer Champagne.

No. 5082-9 oz. Goblet.

Delphian Pattern, Plate Etching No. 272. Blue Foot.

No. 4095–5 oz. Tumbler.

No. 4095–2½ oz. Tumbler

No. 4095½ Candy Jar and Cover

No. 4095½–8 in. Vase.

No. 4095–10 oz. Tumbler.

No. 4095–13 oz. Tumbler.

No. 4095. No. 7 Jug.

Fostoria Glass Company, Moundsville, West Virginia

Made in Crystal, Amber, Blue, Canary and Green.

Fostoria Glass Company, Moundsville, West Virginia.

No. 2297
7 in. Candlestick.

No. 2288
"Tut" Vase.

No. 2311
7 in. Candlestick.
Made in Amber and Green only.

No. 2250
½ Lb. Candy Jar and Cover.

No. 2245
8 in. Candlestick.

No. 2275
9 in. Candlestick.

No. 2267
10 in. Deep Footed Bowl, Rolled Edge.

No. 2275
9 in. Candlestick.

Made in Crystal, Amber, Blue, Canary and Green.
Except as otherwise noted.

Fostoria Glass Company, Moundsville, West Virginia.

No. 2290. 7 in. Plate, Deep Salad.
No. 2290. 8 in. Plate, Deep Salad.
No. 2290. 13 in. Plate, Deep Salad.

No. 4095. 10 in. Large Vase, Flared.
No. 4095. 9 in. Medium Vase, Flared
No. 4095. 8 in. Small Vase, Flared.
Made in Amber, Blue and Green.

No. 2287. Lunch Tray, "Fleur-de-Lis"

No. 4095. Large Vase, Rolled Edge.
Discontinued.

Made in Crystal, Amber, Blue, Canary and Green.
Except as otherwise noted.

Fostoria Glass Company, Moundsville, West Virginia.

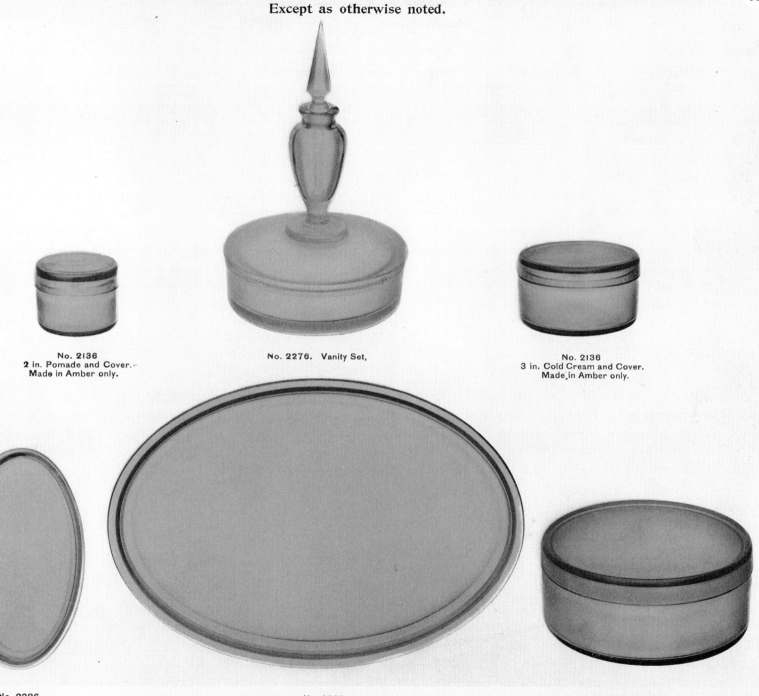

No. 2136
2 in. Pomade and Cover.
Made in Amber only.

No. 2276. Vanity Set,

No. 2136
3 in. Cold Cream and Cover.
Made in Amber only.

No. 2286
5. in, Pin Tray.
Made in Amber and Ebony.

No. 2286
10½ in. Comb and Brush Tray.
Made in Amber and Ebony.

No. 2136
5 in. Bon Bon and Cover.
Made in Amber only.

92

No. 2308. Bobache. Made in Amber only

4 in. Prism.
Made in Amber and Green.

No. 2311. Lustre.
Made in Amber and Green.

No. 2284. Epergne Set
Made in Amber and Green.

No. 2219
½ Lb. Candy Jar and Cover, Amber.

Fostoria Glass Company, Moundsville, West Virginia.

No. 1861½.   6 in. Jelly, Flared.

No. 2297
8 in. Vase, Square Top.
Discontinued

No. 2297½
8 in. Vase, Rolled Edge.

No. 2269. 6 in. Candlestick.   No. 2267. 7 in. Console Bowl.   No. 2269. 6 in. Candlestick.

Made in Crystal, Amber, Blue, Canary and Green.

Fostoria Glass Company, Moundsville, West Virginia.

No. 2297.   10½ in. Deep Bowl "C" Rolled Edge.

No. 2297.   10¼ in. Shallow Bowl "A" Flared.

No. 2297.   7½ in. Shallow Bowl "D" Regular.

No. 2297.   10½ in. Deep Bowl "B" Cupped.

Made in Crystal, Amber, Blue, Canary and Green.
Except Bases and Vases only made in Ebony.

Fostoria Glass Company, Moundsville, West Virginia.

No. 2297½
7½ in. Deep Bowl "D" Regular with Ebony Base.
Replaced by 2339 Bowl, Page 72

No. 1491
6 in. Vase, Ebony.

No. 2297½
9¾ in. Shallow Bowl "C" Rolled Edge with Ebony Base.
Replaced by 2339 Bowl, Page 72

No. 2312
10 in. Vase, Ebony.

No. 2297½
9¾ in. Shallow Bowl "B" Cupped with Ebony Base.
Replaced by 2339 Bowl, Page 72

No. 1491
8½ in. Vase, Ebony.

No. 2297½
12 in. Deep Bowl "A" Flared with Ebony Base.
Replaced by 2339 Bowl, Page 72

Made in Crystal, Amber, Blue, Canary and Green.

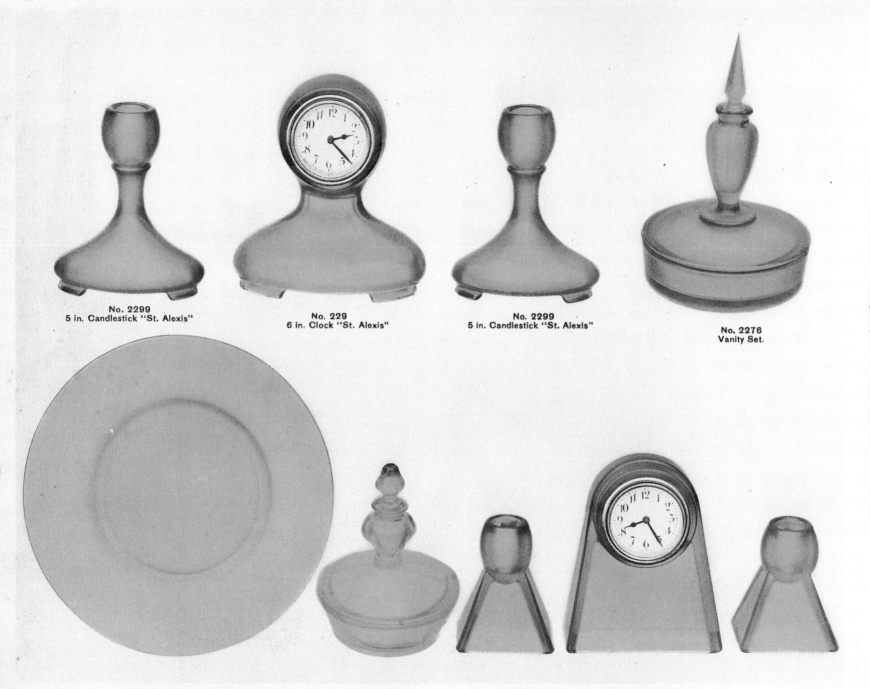

No. 2299
5 in. Candlestick "St. Alexis"

No. 229
6 in. Clock "St. Alexis"

No. 2299
5 in. Candlestick "St. Alexis"

No. 2276
Vanity Set.

No. 2283. 8 in. Salad Plate.
Made also in 6, 7, 9, 11 and 13 in.

No. 2289
Vanity Set.

No. 2298
3½ in. Candlestick "St. Clair"

No. 2298
5 in. Clock "St. Clair"

No. 2298
3½ in. Candlestick "St. Clair"

Fostoria Glass Company, Moundsville, West Virginia.

Fostoria Glass Company, Moundsville, West Virginia

No. 2315. Mayonnaise.

No. 2315. Grape Fruit.

No. 2315. Sugar.

No. 2315. Cream.

No. 2315. 10½ in. Bowl "A" Flared.

No. 2315. 10½ in. Bowl "C" Rolled Edge.

Made in Crystal, Amber, Blue, Canary and Green
Except as noted otherwise.

No. 2255. Sugar.
(Made in Amber and Green only)

No. 2255. Cream.
(Made in Amber and Green only)

No. 2320
10 in. Nappy "B" Cupped and Ebony Base.

No. 2320. 12 in. Nappy "A" Flared.

No. 2330. Sherbet and Plate, (One Piece.)
(Made in Green only)

No. 2315. 11½ in. Bowl "B" Shape.

No. 2315. 8¾ in. Bowl "D" Shape.

Fostoria Glass Company, Moundsville, West Virginia

Fostoria Glass Company, Moundsville, West Virginia

No. 2324. 12 in. Candle.   No. 2324. 13 in. Console Bowl.   No. 2324. 12 in. Candle.

Made in Crystal, Amber, Blue, Canary and Green

No. 2324. 4 in. Candle

No. 2324. 4 in. Candle.

No. 2329. 11 in. Centerpiece.

No. 2324. 9 in. Candle.

No. 2824. Small Urn.
Top Diameter, 7 inches.

No. 2324. 9 in. Candle.

Fostoria Glass Company, Moundsville, West Virginia

Fostoria Glass Company, Moundsville, West Virginia

No. 2341. 8 in. Plate.

No. 2342. 8 in. Plate.

No. 2316. 8 in. Soup Plate.
(Made in Crystal, Amber, Blue and Green)

No. 2333. 11 in. Candle.
No. 2333. 8 in. Candle.
(Made in Crystal and Amber only)

No. 2333. 11 in. Console Bowl.
(Made in Crystal and Amber only)

No. 2333. 11 in. Candle.
(Made in Crystal and Amber only.

No. 2339. 7 in. Console Bowl "D" Regular.

No. 2339. 10 in. Console Bowl "C" Rolled Edge.

No. 2339
10½ in. Console Bowl "A" Flared with Ebony Base.

No. 2439
10½ in. Console Bowl "B" Cupped with Ebony Base.

Fostoria Glass Company, Moundsville, West Virginia

Fostoria Glass Company, Moundsville, West Virginia

No. 2327. 7 in. Comport. Regular.

No. 2327. 7 in. Comport. Salver Shape.

No. 2300. 12 in. Vase.

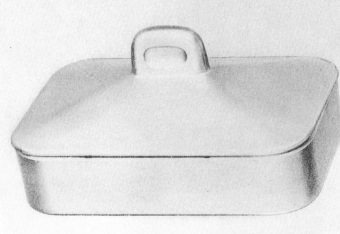

No. 2328. 7 in. Oblong Candy Box and Cover.

No. 2331/3. 7 in. Round Candy Box and Cover.
Divided into Three Compartments.

Made in Green, Amber and Blue Only

Shakers made in all Colors

No. 2321. Sugar.

No. 2111
Shakers, F. G. T.

No. 2128
Shakers, F. G. T.

No. 2127
Shakers, F. G. T.

No. 2321. Cream.

No. 2321. Mayonnaise.

No. 2321. Bouillon.

No. 2321
Footed Custard, Handled.

No. 2321
Footed Tumbler, Handled.

No. 2321   3 Pint Pitcher.

Fostoria Glass Company, Moundsville, West Virginia

Made in Crystal, Amber, Blue and Canary Only

No. 2056. 6 in. Bon Bon.

No. 2056. Hair Receiver.

No. 2056
Small Cigarette and Cover.

No. 2056½. Cologne.

No. 2183. Puff and Cover.

No. 2056
Square Puff and Cover.

No. 2056. Confection and Cover.

No. 2056. 5 in. Pin Tray.

No. 2056. Large Cigarette and Cover.

No. 2056½. 10 in. Comb and Brush Tray.

Fostoria Glass Company, Moundsville, West Virginia

Made in Crystal, Amber, Blue, Canary and Green
Except as noted otherwise

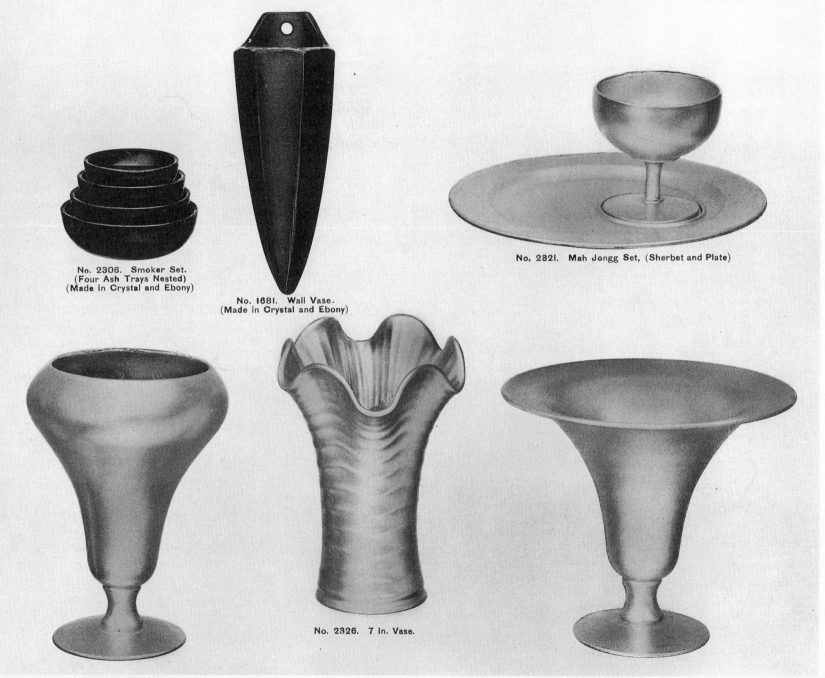

No. 2306. Smoker Set.
(Four Ash Trays Nested)
(Made in Crystal and Ebony)

No. 1681. Wall Vase.
(Made in Crystal and Ebony)

No. 2321. Mah Jongg Set, (Sherbet and Plate)

No. 2326. 7 in. Vase.

No. 2292. 8 in. Vase, Regular.
(Made in Crystal and Green)

No. 2292. 8 in. Vase, Flared.
(Made in Crystal and Green)

Fostoria Glass Company, Moundsville, West Virginia

Made in Crystal, Amber, Blue, Canary, Green and Ebony
Except as noted otherwise.

107

Fostoria Glass Company, Moundsville, West Virginia

No. 2324½. 4 in. Candle.

No. 2329. 14 in. Centerpiece (Made in Green and Ebony only)

No. 3324½. 4 in. Candle.

No. 2297. 10½ in. Shallow Bowl Flared "A"

No. 2320 11 in. Nappy Flared "B"
on 3½ in. Ebony Base.

Colored Lead Blown Ware.

No. 4095. 13 oz. Ftd. Tumbler.
Spiral Optic.

No. 4095. 10 oz. Ftd Tumbler.
Spiral Optic.

No. 5083. 2¾ oz. Wine.
Spiral Optic.

No. 5083. 3 oz. Cocktail.
Spiral Optic.

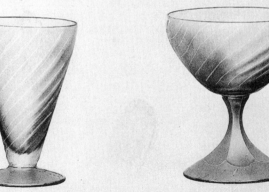

No. 4095. 5 oz. Ftd. Tumbler.
Spiral Optic.

No. 5083. 5½ oz. Fruit.
Spiral Optic.

No. 5083. 5½ oz. Saucer Champagne.
Spiral Optic.

No. 5083. 9 oz. Goblet.
Spiral Optic.

No. 869. 9 oz. Goblet.
Optic.

No. 869. 5½ oz. Saucer Champagne.
Optic.

No. 869. 5½ oz. Fruit.
Optic.

No. 869. 12 oz. Tumbler.
Optic.

No. 4095. 10 oz. Ftd. Tumbler.
Loop Optic.

No. 5082. 5 oz. Fruit.
Loop Optic.

No. 5082. 5 oz. Saucer Champagne
Loop Optic.

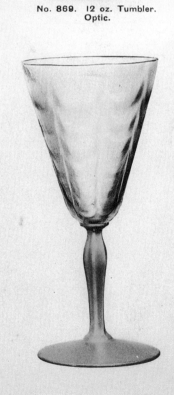

No. 5082. 9 oz. Goblet,
Loop Optic.

Fostoria Glass Company, Moundsville, West Virginia

Colored Lead Blown Ware.

Fostoria Glass Company, Moundsville, West Virginia

No. 4095½. Candy Jar and Cover.
Optic.

No. 5082. 6 oz. Parfait.
Optic.

No. 5082. 2¾ oz. Wine.
Optic.

No. 5082. 3 oz. Cocktail.
Optic.

No. 4095. Oyster Cocktail.
Optic.

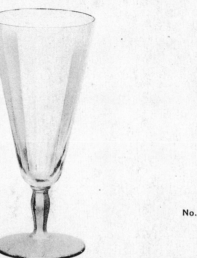

No. 5082. 5 oz. Fruit.
Optic.

No. 5082. 5 oz. Saucer Champagne.
Optic.

No. 5082. 9 oz. Goblet.
Optic.

Colored Lead Blown Ware.
Made in Solid Amber, Blue and Green.
PATENT APPLIED FOR.

Fostoria Glass Company, Moundsville, West Virginia

No. 5084. 12 oz.
Ftd. Tumbler, Optic.

No. 5084. 9 oz.
Ftd. Tumbler, Optic.

No. 5084. 5 oz.
Ftd. Tumbler, Optic.

No. 870. Oyster Cocktail
Optic.

No. 5084. 2½ oz.
Ftd. Tumbler, Optic.

No. 870. 9 oz. Goblet.
Optic.

No. 870. 5½ oz.
Saucer Champagne, Optic.

No. 870. 5½ oz. Fruit, Optic.

No. 870. 3 oz. Cocktail.
Optic.

No. 870. 6 oz. Parfait.
Optic.

Colored Lead Blown Ware.

Fostoria Glass Company, Moundsville, West Virginia

No. 5093. 6 oz. Parfait.
Loop Optic.

No. 5093. 2¾ oz. Wine.
Loop Optic.

No. 5093. 3 oz. Cocktail.
Loop Optic.

No. 5084. Candy Jar and Cover.
Loop Optic.

No. 5093. 9 oz. Goblet.
Optic.

No. 5093. 5½ oz.
Saucer Champagne.
Optic.

No. 5100. Ftd. Shaker. Loop Optic.
SP Top.

No. 5093. 5½ oz. Fruit.
Optic.

No. 5082½. Grape Fruit, Optic.
No. 5082½. G F Liner, Optic.

Fostoria Glass Company, Moundsville, West Virginia

No. 5100. Parfait,
Spiral Optic.

No. 5100. Sherbet,
Spiral Optic.

No. 5100. Oyster Cocktail,
Spiral Optic.

No. 869. Finger Bowl, Optic.
No. 2283. 6 in. Finger Bowl Plate, Optic.

No. 5100. 2½ oz.
Ftd. Tumbler,
Optic.

No. 5100. 5 oz.
Ftd. Tumbler,
Optic.

No. 5100. 9 oz.
Ftd. Tumbler,
Optic.

No. 5100. 12 oz.
Ftd. Tumbler,
Optic.

No. 5100. No. 7
Ftd. Jug,
Optic.

2350 Dinnerware "Pioneer" Pattern.
Made in Crystal, Amber, Blue and Green.
PATENT APPLIED FOR.

No. 2350. 10 in. Baker.
No. 2350. 9 in. Baker.

No. 2350. Butter and Cover

No. 2350. 15 in. Oval Platter.
No. 2350. 12 in. Oval Platter.
No. 2350. 10½ in. Oval Platter.

No. 2350. 6 in. B & B Plate.

No. 2350. 5 in. Fruit.
No. 2350. 6 in. Cereal.

No. 2350. Bouillon and Saucer.
No. 2350. 8 in. Plate.

No. 2350. 7 in. Salad Plate.
No. 2350. 9 in. Dinner Plate.
No. 2350. 10 in. Dinner Plate.

No. 2350. Cup and Saucer.

"Queen Anne" Pattern No. 2412
Made in Crystal, Amber, Blue and Green.

115

Fostoria Glass Company, Moundsville, West Virginia

No. 2412. 14½ in. Lustre & U D Prism.   No. 2412. 9 in. High Foot Bowl.   No. 2412. 14½ in. Lustre & U D Prism.

No. 2412 "Queen Anne" Pattern
Made in Crystal, Amber, Blue and Green.

No. 2412. 11 in. Centerpiece.

No. 2412. 14 in. Vase.
No. 2412. 12 in. Vase.

No. 2412. 9 in. Shallow Low Foot Bowl.

No. 2412. 9 in. Candle.

Fostoria Glass Company, Moundsville, West Virginia

Fostoria Glass Company, Moundsville, West Virginia

No. 2367. 8 in. Bulb Bowl.
Made also in Ebony.

No. 1479. 6 in. Vase.

No. 2360. 8 in. Vase.
No. 2360. 10 in. Vase.

No. 5085. 8 in. Vase.

No. 5086. 9 in. Vase.

No. 5087. 8 in. Vase.

No. 4100. 8 in. Vase.

Cigarettes, Puffs and Colognes.
Made in Crystal, Amber, Blue and Green.

No. 2322. Cologne.
Also made in Ebony.

No. 2347. Puff and Cover.

No. 2322. Cologne.
Also made in Ebony.

No. 2323. Cologne.
Also made in Ebony.

No. 2347½. Puff and Cover.

No. 2323. Cologne.
Also made in Ebony.

No. 2106 Large Cigarette and Cover.

No. 2338. Puff and Cover.

No. 2359½. Puff and Cover.

No. 2349. Cigarette.

No. 2351. Cigarette.
Also made in Ebony.

No. 2351½. Cigarette.

No. 5092. Cigarette.

Fostoria Glass Company, Moundsville, West Virginia

"Arbor" Pattern Cutting No. 184
Made in Amber, Blue and Green.

No. 869. 9 oz. Goblet.   No. 869. 6 oz. Parfait.   No. 869. 5½ oz. Saucer Champagne.   No. 869. 5½ oz. Fruit.

No. 869.   Finger Bowl.
No. 2283. 6 in. Finger Bowl Plate.

No. 5100. 5 oz. Ftd. Tumbler.   No. 5100. 9 oz. Ftd. Tumbler.   No. 5100. 12 oz. Ftd. Tumbler.   No. 5100. No. 7 Ftd. Jug.

Fostoria Glass Company, Moundsville, West Virginia

"Arbor" Pattern Cutting No. 184
Made in Amber, Blue and Green.

No. 2250. ½ Lb. Candy Jar and Cover.

No. 2331 - 3 Candy Box and Cover.

No. 2287. 11 in. Hld. Lunch Tray.

No. 2327. 7 in. Comport.

No. 2324. 4 in. Candle.

No. 2329. 11 in. Centerpiece.
No. 2309. 3¾ in. Flower Block

No. 2324. 4 in. Candle.

Fostoria Glass Company, Moundsville, West Virginia

"Arbor" Pattern Cutting No. 184
Made in Amber, Blue and Green.

121

Fostoria Glass Company, Moundsville, West Virginia

No. 2276. Vanity Set.

No. 2292. 8 in. Vase, Flared.

No. 4100. 8 in. Vase.

No. 2297. 10 in. Shallow Bowl, A

No. 2324. 10 in. Footed Bowl

"Burnswick" Pattern Needle Etching No. 79
Made in Crystal, Amber, Blue and Green.
PATENT APPLIED FOR.

No. 870. 6 oz. Parfait.

No. 870. 2¾ oz. Wine.

No. 870. 3 oz Cocktail.

No. 2283. 7 in. Plate.

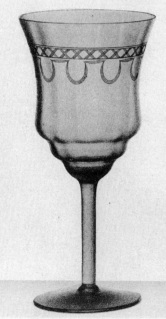

No. 870. 9 oz. Goblet.

No. 870. 5½ oz.
Saucer Champagne.

No. 870. 5½ oz. Fruit.

No. 870. Oyster Cocktail.

Fostoria Glass Company, Moundsville, West Virginia

Royal Pattern, Plate Etching No. 273
Made in Crystal, Amber, Blue and Green.

123

Fostoria Glass Company, Moundsville, West Virginia

No. 2331-3. 7 in. Candy Box and Cover.

No. 2290. 8 in. Plate.

No 2315. 10½ in.
Ftd. Bowl A. Flared.

No. 2324. 4 in. Candle.

No. 2329. 11 in. Centerpiece.
No. 2309. 3¾ in. Flower Block.

No. 2324. 4 in. Candle.

Royal Pattern, Plate Etching No. 273
Made in Crystal, Amber, Blue and Green.

No. 2267. 7 in. Bowl.

No. 2315. Grape Fruit.

No. 1861½. 6 in. Jelly.

No. 2292. 8 in. Vase, Flared.

No. 2327. 7 in. Comport.

Fostoria Glass Company, Moundsville, West Virginia

"Burnswick" Pattern Needle Etching No. 79
Made in Crystal, Amber, Blue and Green.
PATENT APPLIED FOR.

No. 869.   12 oz. Tumbler.

No. 869.   5 oz. Tumbler.

No. 869.   2 oz. Tumbler.

No. 869.   Finger Bowl.
No. 2283.   6 in. Finger Bowl Plate.

No. 869.   Table Tumbler.

No. 5084.   9 oz. Ftd. Tumbler.

No. 5084.   12 oz. Ftd. Tumbler.

No. 5084.   No. 7 Ftd. Jug.

Fostoria Glass Company, Moundsville, West Virginia

"Royal" Pattern Plate Etching No. 273
Made in Crystal, Amber, Blue and Green.
PATENT Nos. 68,424 and 68,425

No. 869.   9 oz. Goblet.

No. 869.   6 oz. Parfait.

No. 869.   5½ oz. Saucer Champagne.

No. 869.   5½ oz. Fruit.

No. 5100.   Ftd. Shaker SP Top.

No. 869.   Finger Bowl.
No. 2283.   6 in. Finger Bowl Plate.

No. 5100.   9 oz.
Ftd. Tumbler.

No. 5100.   5 oz.
Ftd. Tumbler.

No. 5100.   2½ oz.
Ftd. Tumbler.

No. 869.
Table Tumbler.

No. 1236.   No. 6 Jug.

"Royal" Pattern Plate Etching No. 273
Made in Crystal, Amber, Blue and Green.
PATENT Nos. 68,424 and 68,425

127

No. 2350. 10 in. Baker.
No. 2350. 9 in. Baker.

No. 2315. Cream.

No. 2315. Sugar.

No. 2350. 15 in. Oval Platter.
No. 2350. 12 in. Oval Platter.
No. 2350. 10½ in. Oval Platter.

No. 2350. 6 in. B & B Plate.

No. 2350. 5 in. Fruit.
No. 2350. 6 in. Cereal.

No. 2350. Cream Soup.
No. 2350. 7 in. Plate.
No. 2350. 9 in. Plate.

No. 2350. 8 in. Salad Plate.
No. 2350. 10 in. Dinner Plate.

No. 2350. Cup and Saucer.

"Vesper" Pattern Plate Etching No. 275
Made in Amber, Blue and Green.
PATENT APPLIED FOR.

No. 2350. Cream.

No. 2350. 10 in. Baker.
No. 2350. 9 in. Baker.

No. 2350. Sugar.

No. 2350. 15   in. Oval Platter.
No. 2350. 12   in. Oval Platter.
No. 2350. 10½ in. Oval Platter.

No. 2350. 6 in. B & B Plate.

No. 2350. 6 in. Cereal.
No. 2350. 5 in. Fruit.

No. 2350. 7 in. Soup Plate.
No. 2350. 9 in. Plate.

No. 2350. 7 in. Salad Plate.
No. 2350. 8 in. Salad Plate.
No. 2350. 10 in. Dinner Plate.

No. 2350. Cup and Saucer.

Fostoria Glass Company, Moundsville, West Virginia

"Vesper" Pattern Plate Etching No. 275
Made in Amber, Blue and Green.
PATENT APPLIED FOR.

Fostoria Glass Company, Moundsville, West Virginia

No. 2267. 7 in. Bowl.

No. 2287. 11 in. Hld. Lunch Tray.

No. 2327. 7 in. Comport.

No. 2315. Grape Fruit, Mayonnaise or Bon Bon.

No. 2350. Cream Soup.

No. 2324. 10 in. Footed Bowl.

No. 2315. 10½ in. Footed Bowl.

"Vesper" Pattern Plate Etching No. 275
Made in Amber, Blue and Green.
PATENT APPLIED FOR.

No. 5100. 12 oz. Ftd. Tumbler.

No. 5100. 9 oz. Ftd. Tumbler.

No. 5100. 5 oz. Ftd. Tumbler.

No. 5082½. Grape Fruit.
No. 945½. G F Liner.

No. 869. Finger Bowl.
No. 2283. 6 in. Finger Bowl Plate.

No. 5093. 9 oz. Goblet.

No. 5093. 6 oz. Parfait.

No. 5093. 5½ oz.
Saucer Champagne.

No. 5093. 5½ oz. Fruit.

No. 5093. Oyster Cocktail.

Fostoria Glass Company, Moundsville, West Virginia

PRICE GUIDE

All items priced in this guide are in very good to mint condition. This is only a guide and L-W Book Sales assumes no liability for losses or gains in using these prices. These prices may vary from state to state, so keep this in mind when using this price guide. The prices in this guide is an estimate of each piece, prices vary depending on color of glass and quality.

PAGE 1
Top Left & Right: $15-20 pr.
Top Middle: $40-60 w/block
Bottom Left & Right: $20-25 pr.
Bottom Middle: $60-100 w/block

PAGE 2
Top Left: $40-50
Top Right: $60-70
Bottom Left & Right: $25-35
Bottom Middle: $40-60

PAGE 3
Top Left: $30-40
Top Right: $40-50
Middle: $15-25
Middle Right: $20-30
Bottom Left: $30-40
Bottom Right: $50-60 set

PAGE 4
Top Row - Left to Right:
$20-25
$40 set
$15
Middle Row - Left Right:
$25-30
$15
$15
Bottom Left & Right: $30 set
Bottom Middle: $100 w/block

PAGE 5
Top Row - Left to Right:
$50-60 w/ladle
$15
$60-70 w/tongs
Middle: $30
Bottom Row - Left to Right
$12
$20
$15
$20

PAGE 6
Top Left: $50
Top Middle: $60
Top Right: $35
Bottom Left: $45
Bottom Right: $60

PAGE 7
Top Left: $150
Top Right: $125
Bottom Row - Left to Right:
$50-60
$75-85
$75-85

PAGE 8
Top Row - Left To Right:
$15-20
$20 set
$15-20
Middle Row - Left to Right: $10-15
$25 set
Bottom Row - Left to Right:
$20
$15
$15
$15

PAGE 9
Top Left: $12
Top Middle: $40
Top Right: $45
Bottom Row - Left to Right:
$60
$15
$15
$12

PAGE 10
Top Row - Left to Right:
$25
$25
$28
$25
Middle: $30
Bottom Row - Left to Right:
$25
$20
$20
$20

PAGE 11
Top Row - Left to Right:
$10 ea. for all three salt shakers
$40 set of sugar & creamer
Middle Row - Left to Right:
$20
$20

Page 11 continued
$15
$25 set - sherbert and plate
Bottom Row - Left to Right:
$75 - bucket and tongs
$50-75 set
$25 set

PAGE 12
Top Left: $15
Top Right: $20
Middle: $15
Bottom Left: $15
Bottom Right: $50

PAGE 13
Top Row - Left to Right:
$40-50
$35-40 set
$20-30 set
Middle Row - Left to Right
$15
$10
Bottom Row - Left to Right:
$10
$10
$10
$130-160

PAGE 14
Top Row - Left to Right:
$20
$15
$15
$15
Middle: $20
Bottom Row - Left to Right:
$20
$15
$15
$15

PAGE 15
Top Row - Left to Right:
$50 set
$20
$20-30 set
Middle Row: $10
Bottom Row - Left to Right:
$15
$15
$15
$75-100

PAGE 16
Top Row - Left to Right:
$20
$20
$20
$20
Middle Row: $25
Bottom Row - Left to Right:
$20
$15
$15
$15

PAGE 17
Top Row - Left to Right:
$20-25
$50 set
$15
Middle Row - Left to Right:
$15-20 set
$10
Bottom Row - Left to Right:
$8
$10
$12
$75-100

PAGE 18
Top Row - Left to Right:
$35
$30
$25
$25
Bottom Row - Left to Right:
$25
$25
$35
$500-900 (color of glass affects price)

PAGE 19
Top Row - Left to Right:
$100
$150-160
Middle Row - Left to Right:
$40
$25-35
Bottom Row - Left to Right:
$75-125
$25-50

132

PAGE 20
Top Row - Left to Right:
$50-75 set
$30-50 set
$100-200 pair
Middle Row - Left to Right:
$150-250 pair - sugar & creamer
$25-35 pair
Bottom Row - Left to Right:
$25-40
$40-60 pair
$75-125 set

PAGE 21
Top Row - Left to Right:
$250
$35
$50
Middle Row - Left to Right:
$35
$45
Bottom Row - Left to Right:
$375
$350
$160

PAGE 22
Top Row - Left to Right:
$45 Bon Bon
$30-40 Sweetmeat
$25-35 Bouillon & Saucer
2nd From Top Row - Left to Right:
$30-35 Lemon Dish
$25-35 Cereal
Middle Row - Left to Right
$35-50 Whipped cream & Ladle
$200-250 Covered Sugar & Creamer
$125 Ftd. Cheese & Cracker Plate
$50-75 Ftd. Cream Soup & Plate

PAGE 23
Top Row - Left to Right:
$30-45
$45-75 set
$175-200 pair
Middle Row - Left to Right:
$35-45
$25-25
$25-35 Relish
$75-125 Baker
Bottom Row - Left to Right:
$100-150
$75-125 set

PAGE 24
Top Row - Left to Right:
$40
$30

Page 24 continued
$25
$25
Bottom Row - Left to Right:
$25
$25
$30
$400-600

PAGE 25
Top Row - Left to Right
$40-50 pair of candle holders
$85-100 bowl & flower block
Bottom Row - Left To Right:
$75-150 pair of candle holders
$175-200 bowl

PAGE 26
Top Row - Left to Right:
$35
$25
$20
$20
Bottom Row - Left to Right:
$20
$20
$25
$300-500

PAGE 27
Top Row - Left to Right:
$150-250 set
$150-200 set
$125-175 w/cover
Middle Row - Left to Right:
$40
$50-100
$75-125
Bottom Row - Left to Right:
$75-125 pair candle holders
$125-225 bowl w/flower block

PAGE 28
Top Row - Left to Right:
$75-100
$30-50
$75
Bottom Row - Left to Right:
$75-125 pair candle holders
$75-150 bowl

PAGE 29
Top Row - Left to Right:
$75-100
$175-225
$65
Bottom Row - Left to Right:
$80-120
$150-200
$80-120

PAGE 30
Top Row - Left to Right:
$75-100
$75-100
$75
Bottom Row - Left to Right:
$50-75 pair candle holders
$40-60 bowl & flower block

PAGE 31
Top Row - Left to Right:
75-100
$40-60
Middle Row: 40-60
Bottom Row - Left to Right:
$60-80
$50

PAGE 32
Top Row - Left to Right:
$30
$25
$20
$20
Bottome Row - Left to Right:
$20
$20
$25
$150-200

PAGE 33
Top Row - Left to Right:
$25-50 set sugar & creamer
$50
Middle Row: $30
Bottom Row - Left to Right:
$75-100
$75 w/ladle
$75 w/tongs

PAGE 34
Top Row - Left to Right:
$30-50 pair candle holders
$50-75 bowl and flower block
Middle Row: $75 set
Bottom Row - Left to Right:
$30-50 pair candle holders
$50-75 bowl and flower block

PAGE 35
Top Row - Left to Right:
$40-60
$75-100
$50-75
Bottom Row - Left to Right:
$50-75
$50
$75

PAGE 36
Top Row - Left to Right:
$25
$75
$30
Middle Row - Left to Right:
$30 sm cigarette
$50 lg cigarette
Bottom Row - Left to Right:
$60
$45
$80

PAGE 37
Top Row - Left to Right:
$125-175
$75
$75
Bottom Row - Left to Right:
$50-75 pair candle holders
$175-225 centerpiece and flower holder

PAGE 38
Top Row - Left to Right:
$200-300
$250
$200-300
Bottom Row - Left to Right:
$400
$175-200 pair candle holders
$250-300

PAGE 39
Top Row: All are $50-75 ea.
Bottom Row - Left to Right:
$30-70 pair candle holders
$200-250 centerpiece and flower block

PAGE 40
Top Row - Left to Right:
$20
$20
$15
$10
Middle Row - Left to Right:
$75 pair
$30 set, finger bowl and plate
Bottom Row - Left to Right:
$15
$15
$12
$10
$150-200

PAGE 43
Top Row - Left to Right:
$15
$10
$15
$15
Bottom Row - Left to Right:
$10
$10
$15

PAGE 44
Top Row - Left to Right:
$10
$10
$12
$15
$10
$10
$12
$20

PAGE 45
Top Row - Left to Right:
$20
$12
$12
$12
Bottom Row - Left to Right:
$10
$10
$12
$15

PAGE 46
Top Row - Left to Right:
$15
$10
$10
$20
Middle Row: $25 set
Bottom Row - Left to Right:
$10
$10
$10
$50-100

PAGE 47
Top Row - Left to Right:
$15
$20
$15
$15
$30
Bottom Row - Left to Right:
$75-150
$40
$100-200

PAGE 48
$75
$65-75
$80
$65-75
$65-75

PAGE 49
$75-100 set of sugar and creamer
Bottom Row - Left to Right:
$50-60
$60
$65-75
$60
$60

PAGE 50
Top Row: $75-100
Bottom Row - Left to Right:
$75
$75-100
$75-100
$75

PAGE 51
Top Row: $75-100 set
Bottom Row: $100 each piece

PAGE 52
Top Row - Left to Right:
$15
$12
$20
$25
$25
Middle Row: $12
Bottom Row - Left to Right:
$25-35 set
$20
$22
$25-30

PAGE 53
Top Row - Left to Right:
$25-30 set
$25-30 set of sugar and creamer
Middle: $30 set
Bottom Row - Left to Right:
$20
$12
$15
$20

PAGE 54
Top Row - Left to Right:
$25-30 set
$15
$15
$10
Middle: $15 nappy

Page 54 continued
Bottom Row - Left to Right:
$10
$10
$15
$15

PAGE 55
Top Row - Left to Right:
$15-25
$10
$10
Bottom Row - Left to Right:
$10
$10
$15
$100-150

PAGE 56
Top Row: All are $15 each
Bottom Row - Left to Right:
$10
$10
$150-200

PAGE 57
Top Row - Left to Right:
$10
$10
$15
$20
Bottom Row - Left to Right:
$10
$10
$12
$12
$15

PAGE 58
Top Row: All are $6-10 each
Bottom Row - Left to Right:
$10
$12
$10
$15
$10

PAGE 59
Top Row - Left to Right:
$20
$35-50 set
Bottom Row - Left to Right:
$50-75 set
$30-40
$25-30

PAGE 60
Top Row: $35 set of sugar and creamer
Bottom Row - Left to Right:
$35
$25
$50-100

PAGE 61
Top Row - Left to Right:
$15
$15
$15
$17
$17
Middle: $25-35 set
Bottom Row - Left to Right:
$10
$15
$10
$15

PAGE 62
Top Row - Left to Right:
$10
$10
$10
$15
Bottom Row - Left to Right:
All Tumblers $10
Handled Tumbler $15

PAGE 63
Top Row - Left to Right:
$12
$25 set
$35
$20
$25
$25

PAGE 64
Top Row: $175-275
Bottom Row - Left to Right:
$75-100
$150-250

PAGE 65
Top Row - Left to Right:
$25
$20
$25
Bottom Row - Left to Right:
$35
$30
$40

PAGE 66
Top Row - Left to Right:
$15
$15

134

Page 66 continued
$15
$17
$17
Bottom Row - Left to Right:
$10
$15
$10
$15

PAGE 67
Top Row - Left to Right:
$10
$10
$10
$15
Bottom Row - Left to Right:
All Tumblers $10
Handled Tumbler $15

PAGE 68
Top Row - Left to Right:
$50 pair
$30
$35 set for sugar and creamer
Bottom Row - Left to Right:
$25-35
$50
$40
$60

PAGE 69
Left to Right:
$75
$150-200
$175-275

PAGE 70
Top Row - Left to Right:
$15
$15
$12
$12
Bottom Row - Left to Right:
$10
$10
$10
$12
$15

PAGE 71
Top Row - Left to Right:
$10
$10

Page 71 continued
$10
$15
Bottom Row - Left to Right:
All Tumblers $10
Handled Tumblers $15

PAGE 72
Top Row - Left to Right:
$25-30
$20-30
$25-30
Bottom Row - Left to Right:
$35-50
$30-50
$40-50

PAGE 73
Top Row - Left to Right:
$35 set
$45 set
Bottom Row - Left to Right:
$75-100 set
$75-100 set
$100-150

PAGE 74
Top Row - Left to Right:
$50
$45
Bottom Row - Left to Right:
$25
$75
$100-200

PAGE 75
Top Row - Left to Right:
$15
$20
Bottom Row - Left to Right: $20-25 each

PAGE 76
Top Row - Left to Right:
$15
$15
$12
$12
Middle Row: $45 set
Bottom Row - Left to Right:
$10
$10
$10
$12
$15

PAGE 77
Top Row - Left to Right:
$50 pair
$10
$10
$10
$15
Bottom Row - Left to Right:
All Tumblers $10
Handled Tumbler $15

PAGE 78
Top Row - Left to Right
$20
$25 set
$75-100 set
Bottom Row - Left to Right:
$30
$35
$40

PAGE 79
Top Row - Left to Right:
$30-40
$40 set of sugar and creamer
Bottom Row - Left to Right:
$75-100
$75-100 set
$200-300

PAGE 80
Top Row - Left to Right:
$25
$15
$20
$20
$20
Middle Row: $35 set
Bottom Row - Left to Right:
$12
$15
$20
$25

PAGE 81
Top Row - Left to Right:
$25-30
$15
$15
$15
$25
Bottom Row - Left to Right:
$10
$10

Page 81 continued
$10
$10
$12
$25-30

PAGE 82
Top Row - Left to Right:
$20
$35-50 set
$50-75 set
Bottom Row - Left to Right:
$25
$30
$50-60

PAGE 83
Top Row - Left to Right:
$50
$35-45
$50-75 set
Bottom Row - Left to Right:
$200-300
$75-100 set
$250-350

PAGE 84
Top Row - Left to Right:
$25
$15
$20
$20
$20
Bottom Row - Left to Right:
$12
$15
$20
$25

PAGE 85
Top Row - Left to Right:
$15
$20
Bottom Row - Left to Right:
$175-275
$20
$22
$250-350

PAGE 86
Top Row - Left to Right:
$45
$50
Bottom Row - Left to Right:
$50-60
$50-60
$75
$75-100

AGE 87
p Row - Left to Right:
5-50
0
5
ddle Row: $35-45 set
ttom Row - Left to Right:
0
5
0
0

AGE 88
p Row - Left and Right:
5
0
ddle: $50-75
ttom Row - Left to Right:
00-400
0
0
50-450

GE 89
p Row - Left to Right:
5-30 pair
0
5-30 pair
0-60
0-30 pair
ttom Row - Left to Right:
0-30 pair
0-75 ftd. bowl

GE 90
p: $20
ttom Row - Left to Right:
0-75
0-75
0-120

GE 91
p Row - Left to Right:
0
5-125
0-60
ttom Row - Left to Right:
0-60
00
0-60

GE 92
ft to Right:
50-450 pair of Lustre
00-250 Epergne set
5-125 Candy Jar

PAGE 93
Top Row - Left to Right:
$150-200
$40
$100-150
Bottom Row - Left to Right:
$50 set of candlesticks
$50 Console Bowl

PAGE 94
Top Row - Left: $50
Top Row - Right: $45
Bottom Row - Left: $40
Bottom Row - Right: $50

PAGE 95
Top Row - Left to Right:
$50
$25-30
$50
$30-40
Bottom Row - Left to Right:
$50-75
$30-40
$50-75

PAGE 96
Top Row - Left to Right:
$175-275 set of candlesticks and clock
$100-150 vanity set
Bottom Row - Left to Right:
6" - $15
7" - $18
8" & 9" - $20-25
11" & 13" - $25-35
$190-210 vanity set
$180-250 set of candlesticks and clock

PAGE 97
Top Row - Left to Right:
$20
$25
$30-40 set, sugar and creamer
$40-50
$40-50

PAGE 98
Top Row - Left to Right:
$75-100
$30-40 set, sugar and creamer
Middle Row - Left to Right:
$50-100
$25-30
Bottom Row - Left to Right:
$40-50
$25-50

PAGE 99
Left and Right: $25-35 pair candlesticks
Middle: $50-75

PAGE 100
Top Row - Left & Right: $30-50 candles
Top Row - Middle: $75
Bottom Row - Left & Right: $80 candles
Bottom Row - Middle: $50-75

PAGE 101
Top Row: Both Plates $15 each
Middle: $12 Soup Plate
Bottom Row - Left & Right: $35-50 pair
Bottom Row - Middle: $75-100

PAGE 102
Top Row - Left: $30-40
Top Row - Right: $40-50
Bottom Row - Left: $60-70
Bottom Row - Right: $75

PAGE 103
Top Row - Left: $50
Top Row - Right: $60
Middle: $50
Bottom Row - Left: $50-75
Bottom Row - Right: $75-100

PAGE 104
Top Row - Left to Right:
$35 set, sugar & cream
$25 mayonnaise
$15-25 each shaker
Bottom Row - Left to Right:
$20
$20
$20
$100-150

PAGE 105
Hair Receiver - $1000
Bon Bon - $200-250
Small Cigarette & Cover - $50
Cologn - $125-150
Puff and Cover - $75-125
Square Puff and Cover - $150-175
Confection and Cover - $250-300
Pin Tray - $150-175
Large Cigarette and Cover - $800-1000
Comb & Brush Tray - $150-200

PAGE 106
Top Row - Left to Right:
$25 set
$25
$25-30 set
Bottom Row - Left to Right:
$75
$125-175
$75

PAGE 107
Top Row - Left & Right: $25-35 pair
Top Row - Middle: $75
Bottom Row - Left: $45
Bottom Row - Right: $100-175

PAGE 108
Top Row - Left to Right:
$15
$15
$25
$20
Bottom Row - Left to Right:
$15
$15
$15
$20

PAGE 109
Top Row - Left to Right:
$25-35
$20-30
$15-20
$15
Bottom Row - Left to Right:
$20
$20
$20
$30-40

PAGE 110
Top Row - Left to Right:
$50
$30
$25
$20
Bottom Row - Left to Right:
$20
$15
$15
$25-30

PAGE 111
Top Row - Left to Right:
$20
$15
$15
$15
$12
Bottom Row - Left to Right:
$20-25
$20
$15
$15
$20

136

PAGE 112
Top Row - Left to Right:
$25
$30
$30
$75
Middle: $75-100 set
Bottom Row - Left to Right:
$25
$20
$20
$35 set

PAGE 113
Top Row - Left to Right:
$25
$20
$20
$35 set
Bottom Row - Left to Right:
$25
$20
$20
$25
$200-300

PAGE 114
9" Baker - $25-35
10" Baker - $25
Butter & Cover - $75-100
15" Oval Platter - $25
12" Oval Platter - $20
101/2" Oval Platter - $20
B & B Plate - $15
Bouillion and Saucer & Plate - $25 set
5" Fruit - $10
6" Cereal - $14
7" Salad Plate - $10
9" Dinner Plate - $15
10" Dinner Plate - $25
Cup & Saucer - $15

PAGE 115
Left & Right: $400 pair of Lustre & Prism
Middle: $200-300

PAGE 116
Centerpiece - $225-300
14" Vase - $250
12" Vase - $200
Low Foot Bowl - $200
Candle Holder - $300 pair

PAGE 117
Top Row - Left to Right:
$40
$75

Page 117 continued
Bottom Row - Left to Right:
$80-125
$50
$60
$50
$75-100

PAGE 118
Top Row - Left to Right:
$125-175
$75
$125-175
$100-150
$75
$100-150
Middle Row - Left to Right:
$500-800
$75-125
$80-120
Bottom Row: All are $30-60 each

PAGE 119
Top Row - Left to Right:
$25-30
$25
$20
$20
$35 set
Bottom Row - Left to Right:
$15
$15
$20
$175-275

PAGE 120
Top Row - Left to Right:
$80-120
$75-100
Middle Row - Left to Right:
$50
$60
Bottom Row - Left & Right: $40-50 pair
Bottom Row - Middle: $75 w/block

PAGE 121
Top Row - Left to Right:
$75
$100
$80
Bottom Row - Left to Right:
$50
$75

PAGE 122
Top Row - Left to Right:
$20
$15
$15
$15
Bottom Row - Left to Right:
$20
$15
$15
$10

PAGE 123
Candy Box w/cover - $100
Plate - $20
Ftd. Flared Bowl - $50-75
4" Candle holders - $50 pair
Centerpiece & block - $75-100

PAGE 124
Top Row - Left to Right:
$30-50
$40
$50
Bottom Row - Left to Right:
$75-100
$50-75

PAGE 125
Top Row - Left to Right:
$15
$10
$10
$25-35 set
Bottom Row - Left to Right:
$10
$15
$15
$350-500

PAGE 126
Top Row - Left to Right:
$15
$15
$10
$10
Middle Row - Left to Right:
$100 pair
$35 set
Bottom Row - Left to Right:
$15
$15
$10
$10
$225-325

PAGE 127
10" Baker - $50
9" Baker - $40
Cream & Sugar - $50-60
15" Oval Platter - $50
12" Oval Platter - $40
101/2" Oval Platter - $40
B & B Plate - $15
5" Fruit - $15
6" Cereal - $10
Cream Soup, 7" & 9" Plate - $35 set
8" Salad Plate - $25
10" Dinner Plate - $30
Cup & Saucer - $20 set

PAGE 128
10" Baker - $60
9" Baker - $40
Cream & Sugar - $75 set
15" Oval Platter - $75
12" Oval Platter - $50
101/2" Oval Platter - $40
B & B Plate - $25
6" Cereal - $25
5" Fruit - $15
Soup Plate & 9" Plate - $50 set
7" Salad Plate - $25
8" Salad Plate- $25
10" Dinner Plate - $30
Cup & Saucer - $35-50 set

PAGE 129
Top Row - Left to Right:
$40
$50
$40
Middle Row - Left to Right:
$60
$25
Bottom Row - Left to Right:
$50
$40

PAGE 130
Top Row - Left to Right:
$25
$20
$20
$75-100 set
Middle: $35-50 set
Bottom Row - Left to Right:
$60
$40
$30
$25
$15